PRESENTING
Harry Mazer

Twayne's United States Authors Series
Young Adult Authors

Patricia J. Campbell, General Editor

TUSAS 673

Harry Mazer

PRESENTING

Harry Mazer

Arthea J. S. Reed

Twayne Publishers
An Imprint of Simon & Schuster Macmillan
New York

Prentice Hall International
London Mexico City New Delhi Singapore Sydney Toronto

Twayne's United States Authors Series No. 673

Presenting Harry Mazer
Arthea J. S. Reed

Twayne Publishers
An Imprint of Simon & Schuster Macmillan
1633 Broadway
New York, NY 10019

Library of Congress Cataloging-in-Publication Data

Reed, Arthea J. S.
    Presenting Harry Mazer / Arthea J.S. Reed.
        p.   cm. — (Twayne's United States authors series. Young adult authors)
    Includes bibliographical references (p.   ) and index.
    ISBN 0-8057-4512-2 (cloth)
    1. Mazer, Harry—Criticism and interpretation.   2. Young adult fiction, American—History and criticism.   I. Title.   II. Series.
PS3563.A9816Z84   1996
813'.54—dc20   96-23992
                                                                                        CIP

10 9 8 7 6 5 4 3 2 1 (hc)

Printed in the United States of America.

To Verna E. Bergemann,
mentor and friend

Contents

Foreword

The advent of Twayne's Young Adult Author Series in 1985 was a response to the growing stature and value of adolescent literature and the lack of serious critical evaluation of the new genre. The first volume in the series was heralded as marking the coming-of-age of young adult fiction.

The aim of the series is twofold. First, it enables young readers to research the work of their favorite authors, and to see them as real people. Each volume is written in a lively, readable style and attempts to present in an attractive, accessible format a vivid portrait of the author as a person.

Second, the series provides teachers and librarians with insights and background material for promoting and teaching young adult (YA) novels. Each of the biocritical studies is a serious literary analysis of one author's work (or one subgenre within YA literature), with attention to plot, structure, theme, character, setting, and imagery. In addition, many of the series writers delve deeper into the creative writing process by tracking down early drafts or unpublished manuscripts by their subject authors, consulting with their editors or other mentors, and examining influences from literature, film, or social movements.

Many of the contributing authors of the series are among the leading scholars and critics of adolescent literature. Some are even YA novelists themselves. Each study is based on extensive interviews with the subject author and an exhaustive study of his or her work. Although the general format for the series is the same, the individual volumes are uniquely shaped by their subjects, and each brings a different perspective to the classroom.

The goal of the series is to produce a succinct but comprehensive study of the life and art of every leading YA writer, as well as to trace how that art has been accepted by readers and critics; to evaluate its place in the developing field of adolescent literature; and—perhaps most important—to inspire reading and rereading of this ficton, which speaks so directly to young people about their life experiences.

PATRICIA J. CAMPBELL, GENERAL EDITOR

Preface

As Harry Mazer and I walk out of the Gramercy Park Hotel on a clear, cold March morning, I think how strangely out of place he seems in the city—with his blue jeans, plaid flannel shirt, salt-and-pepper beard, horn-rimmed glasses, and hiking boots. This man who cares deeply about others, who called to make sure I was safe and comfortable in my hotel room, does not seem to fit on Manhattan's heartless streets. He is a gentle, quiet man who is sometimes difficult to hear over the noises of the city. Perhaps this explains why so much of his world is internal.

He calls his inner world a gift he possesses. His gift places stories and voices inside his head and allows him to do what he loves and fears most—write books, books with authentic voices and characters who have their own important inner lives. Today, Mazer reveres his own inner life and believes that it is our inner lives that connect us one to the other.

It took him much of a lifetime to realize "what a gift and treasure it is to hear a character's voice" (interview with author, 3 March 1995). For years, he did not appreciate his gift. In fact, he struggled with himself constantly about using it. Writing was not "real work," not the work of workers. Labor was the work that allowed his parents to leave Poland only 20 years before the Holocaust and raise a family in the new world. Labor was the work that would help him change the world. At least, that is what he believed as an idealistic young man. He was torn between his inner world of voices, books, and ideals and what he saw as the real world of hard work and tradition.

Harry Mazer is a man of two worlds—a city world and a country world. I visited him in his city world, the world in which he sets most of his books. He and his wife of 45 years, the author

Norma Fox Mazer, spend 4 months of each year in an apartment in lower midtown Manhattan, a few blocks from Gramercy Park, about an hour's subway ride from the Bronx community where he grew up. Harry Mazer lives in the city, whether he is in it or not, and his mind is shaped by the city. He has an urban mentality made up of buildings, streets, sidewalks, alleys, hallways, hedges, corners, rooftops, cellars, and, most of all, places to hide. He doesn't see danger in the city, unless it is the danger of being on a rooftop. He remembers once a long time ago seeing a man fall off a city roof. Thinking about it still makes him shiver. The dangers he sees are the dangers of his other world, his wintry country world—open, windswept plains and frozen lakes with no places to hide.

The Mazers' home in Jamesville, New York, is next to a dairy farm, tucked against the side of a wooded ravine. Mazer loves being surrounded by trees and looking out over a stream and a dirt road. The sounds of his country home are a comforting juxtaposition to the noise of the city. He writes that often the only sounds he and Norma hear are made by crows and wind in the trees. Increasingly, the land around their home has become garden. "Gradually," says Mazer, "we've worked our way up the hill to the fields where the farmer once plowed." For 16 years the Mazers have been "planting trees and shrubs and flowers and cutting paths, transforming the once bare fields into a parklike garden" (letter to the author, 2 October 1995).

When the Mazers' four children were young, they had dogs and cats, but more cats than dogs. He recalls that at one point they had a pair of breeding Siamese cats. "Cheetah was a wonderful clever cat, Sam was a goofball, a broadfaced, blue eyed, bluepoint, given to terrors that sent him climbing the venetian blinds. We once had seventeen cats in the house at one time," recalls Mazer (letter to the author, 2 October 1995).

Whether in the country or in the city, Harry Mazer is at home in the world of books, an internal world. However, with both his wife, Norma, and his daughter Anne now sharing their writing with each other, this world, too, has become increasingly open and social.

Although a very private man, Harry Mazer is also very forthcoming. I met with him for almost 10 hours on a cold, clear day in March 1995. Norma Mazer joined us, after a morning of writing, for a long lunch and a conversation about Harry, his books, and their relationship. Letters have flown back and forth between his city and country home and my home and office. He has opened his files about his books to me. He has made available reviews of his books and unpublished speeches he has given. I have read his correspondence with readers and with critics. He has answered every question I have asked, except for the birthdays of his children, which he cannot remember. His good humor helped us delve into some difficult issues, and his thoughtful reflection allowed me to probe into his most private thoughts and memories. When a book is published or a written story is shared, the author is exposing himself or herself to all who read it. However, few authors are willing to open their hearts. Harry Mazer is not only an exceptional writer of outstanding young adult books but also an extraordinary human being. He cares about his work, his family, and his readers. Because he cares so deeply, he has been willing to share himself with all of us. I am deeply grateful, and I know that when you read about him and his work, you, too, will come to understand the warmth, kindness, and thoughtful intelligence of the man.

Every book is a team effort. First, I need to thank my home team. My husband, Don, has been more than patient as I have spent hours at the computer rather than at his side. The student assistants in my office at the University of North Carolina at Asheville have helped me locate books, articles, and other material. Most particularly I want to thank Celine Brown, Nikki Honeycutt, and Amy Nix for the many times they traveled the path between office and library. And, of course, my wonderful assistant Judy Carver has helped me make phone calls and transcribe a very long series of cassette-taped interviews and has copied and typed when necessary. Finally, Patty Campbell is an excellent editor. She is gentle in her criticism and always provides guidance when suggesting changes that need to be made. She has helped make the process pleasant and almost easy.

Chronology

1925   Harry Mazer is born on 31 May in New York City to Sam and Rose Mazer.

1939–1943   Attends Bronx High School of Science.

1943   Enlists in U.S. Army Air Forces; serves in Europe as an aerial gunner.

1945   Plane is shot down over Pilzen, Czechoslovakia, 25 April, on his 26th mission.

1946   Meets Norma Fox, age 15.

1948   Receives B.A. in English from Union College.

1950   Marries Norma Fox; moves to Schenectady, New York; works as a welder on the railroad, in a steel mill, and in an auto plant.

1953   Daughter Anne born.

1955   Moves to Passaic, New Jersey. Son Joseph born.

1957–1959   Becomes an English teacher at Central Square High School, Central Square, New York.

1958   Daughter Susan born.

1959   Denied a position in the Syracuse school system because of politics.

1959   Returns to work as a welder.

1960   Receives M.A. in English Education from Syracuse University.

1963   While welding to earn a living, begins to write regularly. Daughter Gina born.

1964   Becomes full-time freelance writer, writing articles and pulp fiction for magazines.

1972   *Guy Lenny.*

1973   *Snow Bound;* made into an NBC After School Special movie.

1974   *The Dollar Man.*
       The Solid Gold Kid, with Norma Fox Mazer.

1978   *The War on Villa Street.*

1979   *The Last Mission.*

1981   *The Island Keeper.*
       I Love You, Stupid!

1984   *Hey, Kid! Does She Love Me?*

1985   *When the Phone Rang.*

1986   *Cave under the City.*

1987   *The Girl of His Dreams.*

1988   *City Light.*

1989   *Heartbeat,* with Norma Fox Mazer.

1990   *Someone's Mother Is Missing.*

1992   *Bright Days, Stupid Nights,* with Norma Fox Mazer.

1993   *Who Is Eddie Leonard?*

1994   Visits the Czech Republic; gives a speech near site of his 1945 crash.

1. Harry Mazer: A Country Man in the City

For Harry Mazer's parents, Sam and Rose Mazer, the new world was as much like the old world as they could make it. They lived in a social and economic community in the Bronx called "the co-ops," a cooperative apartment complex that is the setting for Mazer's *Cave under the City*. It was a community of Jewish, Polish, and Russian immigrants who worked together in the garment factories. Many of the residents had known one another in the old world, and they formed their own clubs and organizations in the new. They shared common values, traditions, work, and religion, and their lives. They brought "Europe over here—right here in New York. You had Jewish theater; you had the Jewish newspapers, Jewish choruses and orchestra."[1] This was the world of Jewish culture in which Mazer grew up—a world that valued tradition and labor, a world that did not encourage a young idealist to honor his gift of voices and an inner life.

In many ways, even in the new world, Mazer's parents were of two separate worlds. His mother was illiterate. Like many young Polish immigrants, she had received no formal education. It was Harry who helped her learn how to read. Ironically, Rose Mazer was the parent who helped young Harry enlarge his inner world by exposing him to theater, concerts, and the world of books that were largely closed to her.

Mazer's father, on the other hand, loved books and stories, but the idea of his son's becoming a writer was foreign to his work ethic and way of life. He often told his son that he was ruining his eyes by reading so much.[2]

1

Does Being American Mean
Not Being Jewish?

Young Harry was torn between the European, Jewish working world and his own inner world. He denied both for many years. It is curious that Mazer, who grew up in a world of Jewish immigrants, has never dealt with being Jewish in one of his books. It's not so much that he denies his Jewishness but that he has lived in what he considers to be a non-Jewish world most of his adult life.

As a boy, Mazer never felt that being Jewish was an issue. He wasn't in a strange world because he was a Jew; his world was Jewish. In fact, he spoke only Yiddish until he was about 4. However, he distinguishes his culturally Jewish world from the religiously Jewish world of his grandparents. You don't have to be religious to be Jewish—the world tells you you are a Jew—you are a part of a discriminated-against minority, says Mazer. His parents' break from the old world was not cultural but religious. Their lives were "anti-Jewish-establishment" (interview with author). They were breaking away from the hold of the rabbi and the synagogue rather than from the old-world Jewish culture that surrounded and protected them in their New York City neighborhood.

Mazer says that he was always aware of anti-Semitism and recognized that he lived in a hostile world with a great deal of discrimination against Jews. When he visited family outside the city, he observed discrimination. Some of his family members were denied jobs because they were Jews, and he remembers seeing billboards advertising hotels that said "Gentiles only" and ads in the classified section of the *New York Times* saying the same. Although such anti-Semitism rarely intruded into his life, it convinced him, even as a boy, that you have to work really hard to make your way.

The Affliction of Having Many Talents

Harry Mazer is a man of contradictions. He recognized early that he had to work hard to make his way, but he also wished that he could do just one thing really well. "Then," he says, "I would know what I would do" (interview with author). Mazer was a good student; he could write; he was a musician, and he and his friends from the Bronx High School of Science formed a science club that met in the cellar of the buildings where they lived. But he was torn: His mother wanted him to go to college, while his father wanted him to become a cutter in the garment industry. Mazer remembers a friend who was gifted in mathematics whose father was a barber. His father wanted him to learn a trade, and so the son went to printing school rather than to an academic high school. Mazer was angry that his friend was wasting his brains and ability. However, the only reason he himself chose to go to Bronx Science was because his friends did. He was good in science but not particularly interested in it. He wanted to be a writer or, perhaps, a musician. When it came time to go to college, he had no idea what he wanted to do, but he enrolled because his friends did. Mazer lasted one day at City College, which was then a free college for qualified students from New York City. Then, despite his mother's objections, he enlisted in the Army Air Corps.

This man of so many talents is still incredibly modest. It is only in the last decade, after 17 books, that he has thought of himself as a writer. Over a breakfast of oatmeal, wheat toast, and decaffeinated coffee, he told me of his struggle not only to become a writer but also to believe that he is one. Finally, at age 70, he is confident in his ability to write. He still has his moments of doubt, however. He says that there has always been a war going on within him. Negativity and denial are not uncommon, but I've felt them quite strongly. . . . It made it difficult for me to write in the beginning, but I think that the fact that I have persisted, and I've lasted, and I've produced, and I know I can write a book. . . . I wasn't convinced I could write early on, not at all! But I don't feel that any more. I'm very strongly connected with the voice of the character—very, very happy when a voice begins to emerge in my head" (interview with author).

It is this authenticity of the voices of his characters that makes Mazer's books connect with young readers. "When the voice is right it's like something outside myself that I can sit back and admire. It's just there, and it can't be any other way." This is what makes good literature for young readers or adult readers: "You feel, you identify, you put yourself into the other person's life, into their skin. This is what I am reaching for—to feel the authenticity of the inner life" (interview with author).

It is also a sense of place that makes Mazer's books come alive. The places are usually urban, but sometimes they are in his other world—his country world. When you meet Mazer, you assume it is the country world that forms the man. He looks more at home in the country than in the city. The Mazers spend the warmer months of the year in their country home outside of Jamesville, New York, or in their camp in Canada. He speaks of their country home and hates to see peaceful summers pass so quickly.

Although Mazer is comfortable in the country, it does not shape him. "My mind is a city mind. . . . But I love the country, and that's why . . . we stay in Jamesville. . . . I love the land" (interview with author). He sets some of his stories on this land—a land that is beautiful and peaceful in the summer but can be very dangerous when the snows and winter winds whip across the plains and the lakes.

The Father and the Son

Harry Mazer, born on 31 May 1925 in New York City, was the first child of Rose and Sam Mazer. His childhood, although filled with contradictions, was a happy one. One of these contradictions was his relationship with his father—a man Harry desperately wanted to know but found stiff and unloving. Harry's father was "a distant, silent man who went to work in a garment factory every morning and came home every night to make his supper and then sit with his newspaper and books."[3]

Although his mother was illiterate, Mazer calls her the story-teller of the family. He speaks of always loving her. She is the mother in his novels *The Dollar Man, I Love You, Stupid!,* and *The Last Mission.* "I've always written my mother," he says. She took him to see plays and concerts, and she worked as a union organizer, a shop steward in the International Ladies Garment Workers Union. Because she worked, she had money, and she did with her earnings what she pleased. She bought new furniture to replace the still-good furniture in their small, two-room apartment. "She drove my father crazy," Mazer says (interview with author). His mother died in the 1970s. His father, who lived another 25 years, never, in all that time, voluntarily said a word to his son about her or about their life together.

Mazer's relationship with his father was always a difficult one. Ironically, it is this relationship that has occupied much of his thought and much of our conversation about his childhood. He has explored difficult father-son relationships in many of his novels. So, although he always writes his mother, it is Mazer's struggle to understand his father that frames the plots of many of his novels.

Perhaps because of this difficult relationship Mazer created the "idyllic father" in his first book, *Guy Lenny*. "At the beginning, when Guy was on the river with his father, I was remembering when I was fishing with my uncle on the Hudson River." Mazer can't remember his own father ever doing anything with him. "Well," he reflects, "we did a few things I remember. We once swam in a quarry, and once when he was seventy he climbed a mountain with me" (interview with author). His father was in good physical condition and stayed in good health almost until he died. Initially Mazer was surprised by the ending of *Guy Lenny*, when Guy's seemingly perfect father betrays him. But today he recognizes that he was merely writing from his own experiences.

Mazer has written several novels about young men seeking their fathers. Marcus in *The Dollar Man* and Eddie in *Who Is Eddie Leonard?* search for the fathers they never knew. Unlike Marcus's and Eddie's fathers, however, Mazer's "was there in my life. He was there every night. He didn't go places. He worked. He was steady as a rock." Mazer says he never knew his father: "He was so tight. He was so ungiving of himself and, so, I never knew" (interview with author).

Mazer's father was never pleased with his son. The last thing he wanted was for his boy to become a writer. Sam Mazer—like

Willis's father in *War on Villa Street* and *The Girl of His Dreams*—entered the United States by walking across the bridge from Canada to Michigan with only a lunch pail and the clothes on his back. "My father," says Mazer, "wasn't an American; he was a Polish Jew. He spoke with an accent. He spoke Yiddish. He was always formally dressed. There was no such thing as going around like this," Mazer says as he points to his blue jeans and plaid flannel shirt. "He always had his suit on; shoes were polished—tie. It was the way to dress. I never in my life, to the day he died at age ninety-six, dressed to please or satisfy him. I never looked right. He didn't play ball; he didn't know anything about ball games. It was not his life" (interview with author).

Like several of his male protagonists, Mazer found a mentor to substitute for the father he did not know—a man named Joe Keen, who was a friend of the family. Mazer thought of Keen as being more American than his father, even though he, too, was Jewish. Joe Keen was from Chicago, a much more American city than New York, and he was born in this country. He was "sort of a mechanic and very clever with machines." Keen was entirely different from Mazer's father. He was very easygoing; nothing disturbed him. He liked to go to ball games and to look at *Esquire* magazine, the *Playboy* of the day: "Everything about Joe was right" (interview with author).

A World of Books

Although Mazer's father read a great deal and his mother told stories and took her son to plays, there were few books in Harry Mazer's house. His family members, with the exception of his father, were not readers. They were house painters, peddlers, shopkeepers, factory workers, chicken farmers, and secretaries, and none of them were readers. But young Harry was a reader with a passion for books. One of the great moments of his young life was getting a library card, and a "transition moment" was going into the adult section of the library. "I know that at one point or another when I was young I was out to read every book [in the library]. I never got very far with it."[4] He recalls reading series books like *Dr. Doolittle* and then reading the classics:

> When I was young, I gobbled up books.
>
> I wanted to read every book by every author: American, English, Russian, French, Irish. I didn't read books so much as authors. I read all of Dostoyevsky, most of Tolstoy, Maxim Gorki. I liked the Russians.
>
> I also read every American novel I could lay my hands on—above all, those of Thomas Wolfe. I loved his enormous, verbose novels. I identified with his artistic hero—admired the man's sensitivity, his appetite for life, his exuberance and rages. I was going to be that artist. I was going to dazzle the world.[5]

According to Mazer, the size of a book never daunted him: "I plunged into Tolstoy's bulky *War and Peace*. I read only for story. My eyes skidded over lengthy descriptions and philosophical ruminations. It's only as I grew older that I became interested in meaning and symbolism and the realistic treatment of character."[6] Each week in the *New York Post* there was a coupon to buy a book for a dollar. With these coupons Mazer's father brought home books by Charles Dickens and Mark Twain. Harry read them all. "I read," he says. "I didn't write. I read" (interview with author).

Of Cellars and Friends

It was this early reading that helped develop Mazer's inner world. And this, woven among the fibers of his real life, provided the fabric for his novels. In his real world, he loved to climb out on the fire escape of their apartment and go over the roof.

The co-ops—the projects where he grew up—had lots of places to play and lots of children to play with. The community was social-minded. The kids formed clubs—sports clubs and science clubs. They set up club rooms in the cellars, built tables, salvaged old couches, had meetings, and did experiments. The cellars are a part of Mazer's city world, as were the abandoned buildings nearby: "I played in that burned-out restaurant [in *Cave under*

the City] and let myself down into the cellar on the dumbwaiter."
And even today these settings loom large in his imagination.

"My friends," Mazer says, "were mostly interested in science.
One was going to be an electrical engineer, another a chemist, a
third a dentist. I said I'd like to be a scientist and went to the
Bronx High School of Science" (interview with author). However,
although he may not have recognized it at the time, he really
dwelled in his inner world rather than in the world of the lab-
oratory.

Of Girls

Mazer made friends easily, but girls were another matter. The
difficulty he had in relating to girls has influenced the plots and
authenticity of the male characters in many of his novels. Mazer
remembers with humor and wit every encounter he ever had with
a girl. That's not too hard, he chuckles, since he didn't talk to
girls, went to an all-male high school, never had a friend who was
a girl, enlisted in the army at 17, and then went to an all-male college. His first real, serious girlfriend was Norma Fox. He met her
when he was 21 and she was 15. It was 2 years before they began
to date. Harry says of the girls who torment the male protagonists
in his novels, "Those are the incidents in my life" (interview with
author).

> I was furtively aware of girls from the sixth grade on. All that
> year I followed Isabel from afar. And, years later, it was Isabel I
> wrote about when I began writing [in the opening of *The Dollar
> Man]. . . .* [As an adolescent] I didn't know how to talk to girls.
> Near girls I kept my head high (the opening of *I Love You,
> Stupid!)* or I kept my nose in a book. I was given to carrying big
> books with impressive titles like Karl Marx's *Das Kapital.*

Harry didn't date in high school, and he didn't talk to girls:
"When girls weren't looking (were they looking?) I looked. I
didn't date in high school. Dating was so complicated, and I
lacked every social skill. I didn't dance. I didn't know how to

small-talk. I got red and embarrassed just standing near a girl. What would I do alone with a girl? What would we talk about? What did you say to a girl?"[7]

Since he rarely talked to girls, it was from books that his knowledge of girls came: "I loved the girls in *War and Peace,* and I identified with these characters. I put myself into these stories, so my relationships with girls were more literary than real life" (interview with author). Ironically, it was literature that attracted Norma Fox to him. They met in Schenectady, New York, after World War II. He was a veteran attending Union College. She was a high school sophomore.

On the day Norma and Harry met, he and a friend were working on a car. When Mazer came out from under the car, Norma was standing there—she had come to Schenectady to visit her sister. His friend told Mazer that it could have been him whom Norma first saw, him whom she feel in love with. Mazer laughs and says, "Of course he was dreaming. It would never have been him. He didn't have a chance. I liked her right away." He liked her so much that he drove her to her home 50 miles away. During that ride they talked of books and ideas: "We had a literary discussion for an hour in the car. She was a reader, and I was a reader. This was what drew us together." When Harry got Norma home, he met her mother: "I saw her nose turn green. I was too old; Norma was too young—only a sophomore in high school" (interview with author). But Mazer didn't forget Norma; he waited 2 years before they began to date; and then, only a little more than a year later, they married.

Of Dreams and Poses

Harry Mazer was an idealist: "I dreamed of making the world a better place."[8] As a young man he dreamed of being a writer. However, for many years, he didn't write at all, unless you count school writing, which he doesn't. But at Bronx Science, Mazer did pose as a writer. His friend Leo was a writer, too, and had proof: He carried a notebook in his pocket. "It was only later that it occurred to me that I never saw [Leo] write anything. I was always buying notebooks—notebooks of different sizes, the kinds that fit into your pocket. I called them journals, diaries, workbooks, and I liked all those names. They gave me the feeling I was really doing something, but of course what I really had, finally, was a fine collection of empty notebooks" (interview with author).

Mazer loved the idea of writing, of self-discipline, order, and routine—all of the things he didn't have. He wanted to write but did not know how. He gives this sense of frustration to his 17-year-old protagonist, Marcus, in *I Love You, Stupid!* Marcus, like young Harry Mazer, wants to be a writer. Unlike Mazer, he does some writing and even has limited success publishing his work. However, Marcus spends most of his time posing as a writer rather than being one—setting up his room so he can write, making lists, sharpening his pencil, telling everyone he is a writer, and then having to face their criticisms when he has only lists to show for his time.

As a teenager Mazer, too, had lots of plans for becoming a writer, but most of these plans were merely posing. The fourth-floor walk-up apartment in which he lived was small for a family of four; there were only two rooms, which made it difficult to write when everyone was home.

> My plan was . . . I'd write till everyone came home. Another plan was—skip food, I was too fat anyway, and I'd just write. I'm thinking of this as I'm going up the stairs, and as I'm going up the stairs I get more and more rigorous. "This is what I'm going to do. This is the first day of my new regimen. Let's go Marcus, I mean Harry. And you're going to lose weight. You're going to get slim. Right? You're going to be famous. Dotty isn't going to be able to keep her hands off you." I unlock the door, and I go straight to the refrigerator (only it's an ice-box). And all that planning had exhausted me. I felt weak. I said, "I'll eat first, and then I'll write."[9]

When Harry wasn't posing as a writer, he was posing as something else. During his "revolutionary phase," he loved to carry around big books like Karl Marx's *Das Kapital*. He also wore work clothes and heavy boots, hoping people would think he was a member of the proletariat. Some days he'd sit on the subway and pose as a musician, playing an imaginary piano. "I'd be carried away. Sometimes, I'd play the cello. There was no instrument too difficult" (Illinois Librarians). Later, when he was in the army, he'd come home on furlough and would pose as a wounded veteran, limping a little. "I was never too old to pose" (Illinois Librarians).

> I remember once, just after Norma and I were married, we were living in New York City—she could only stand it for four months—I was sitting on the subway returning from work. I'd been painting, and I had red paint on my hands and clothes. Sitting across from me I saw Theodore Dreiser—or I thought I saw him—and I thought he was taking notes. Immediately, I began to scowl, and I shoved my hands in my pockets. I had this kind of brooding young sensitive worker look, and I became a character I thought would fit one of his books. I thought he noticed that blood (the paint) on my hands, and I'd be another of his characters, another *American Tragedy*. (Illinois Librarians)

And War and Reality

Mazer's world of dreams and posing led him into the Army Air Corps in World War II. He's not quite sure why he enlisted. It may be that he wasn't ready for college. It may be that he was still conflicted. How could he acknowledge dreaming of being a writer, or posing as a writer, when he believed that it was through labor that the world would change? How could he become a writer, when his father kept telling him to get a trade—that reading would ruin his eyes and that writing would never support a family? Or maybe it was because he was trying to find out what it means to be a man:

> From the time I was in sixth grade, I wondered what it meant to act like a man. . . . In adolescence, as I began defining myself, I felt that whatever I was, I wasn't my father. . . . Whatever he was, I told myself, I was the opposite. If he was quiet, a man of

routine and modest expectations, I was exuberant, ambitious, with big plans. I found my models in the movies. John Garfield with a cigarette in the corner of his mouth, Humphrey Bogart, another tough guy, and John Wayne, rough and indomitable— these were my heroes. They taught me that a man was coura- geous, stood his ground, didn't desert his comrades. A man turned defeat into victory. ("Two Boys," 2)

And, so, at age 17, Harry Mazer, filled with musings about what it means to be a man and filled with idealism about saving the world, enlisted to fight Hitler, to "do something he'd never forget." He dreamed of being a pilot, a navigator, maybe even a bombardier. Reality fell short of his dreams. He "washed out" of officers' training and became an aerial gunner. During his entire tour of duty, he never fired a gun. By April 1945, the war was nearly over; the Germans were without the fuel needed to put fighter planes in the air. Mazer and his best friend, radio opera- tor Mike Brennan—a pale, freckled, redheaded Irish boy from the Bronx—talked of home and girlfriends. The flights that Mazer and his crew took to bomb targets over eastern Europe were deadly dull, noisy, and endless. Mazer often had to fight to stay alert and awake. The only thing that helped was the harness on the emergency chest pack, which had to be strapped so snugly and tightly around his legs that he was unable to stand up straight. As the crew had been warned, if the packs were not secure and the men were forced to jump, they might never be able to have children.

One day after 25 missions and several close calls, the crew was put on alert. They hadn't flown for two weeks. The Allied armies were deep inside Germany, and the Russians were nearing Berlin. The men were kept busy on the base, digging ditches and policing the grounds. Their twenty-sixth mission was to bomb the Skoda munitions factories in Pilzen, Czechoslovakia. They didn't know on that late April morning that this mission would be any differ- ent from the others. But when they approached their target, the sky was already dirty with flak. The clouds kept the crew from dropping the bombs on the first pass. They circled back. On the second approach, the plane was hit by an antiaircraft shell that exploded under the starboard wing and blew half of it off. The plane went out of control:

> I was thrown off my feet, my intercom and oxygen lines were torn loose, and I was pinned against the side of the ship. The plane was tipping and falling. I crawled to the emergency door, but I couldn't get it open. Mike Brennan was in the doorway of the radio compartment [no more than a few feet separated Mike and Harry], a frozen look on his face. O'Malley, another gunner, had come up from the ball turret and was crowding me. My back was to the door. I threw myself against it and fell out of the plane. ("Two Boys," 3)

Mazer—a man who still shivers when he thinks of falling or jumping off a rooftop—had never jumped before and knew what to do only from reading about it:

> I didn't pull my chute right away. We were at 26,000 feet when we were hit, and I probably fell a mile, maybe as much as two. Then I was in the clouds and, unsure how close the ground was, I pulled the handle. The chute snapped open and I blacked out. ("Two Boys," 4)

When he came to, he was drifting slowly toward earth. The day was surprisingly beautiful—not a plane was in sight. He saw a black pillar of smoke in the distance and two other parachutes nearby. He believed that one was O'Malley and the other was the tail gunner. Someone was shooting at him from the ground, and moments after he landed in a field, he was captured. As he saw two Luftwaffe soldiers coming over a hilltop with their guns pointed at him, he put his hands up and called, "Kamerad," an action and a word he knew from having read *All Quiet on the Western Front*.

Mazer and O'Malley were the only survivors. For 50 years, he has wondered if he could have saved Mike Brennan: "I think I'm thinking of nothing, and I find myself thinking: Was I too quick? Did I jump too soon? Did I do right? Did I act like a man?" ("Two Boys," 1).

Mazer and O'Malley were taken prisoner and moved with the retreating Germans toward Austria. At the end of the war, they were in Austria in a Wehrmacht ski troop camp on the Enns River, on the Russian side. In panic, the Germans abandoned them and fled, leaving six prisoners in a locked lecture room. Mazer climbed out of a window; a German officer handed him a pistol. The prisoners commandeered a car and were saluted out of the camp. The roads were clogged with German soldiers abandoning their weapons. The prisoners drove slowly toward the American lines. Mazer felt free and alive—as though another life had been given to him. But for 50 years he wondered whether he had abandoned Mike Brennan—wondered whether he had acted like a man. War had not taught him what it is to be a man.

Mazer has written *The Last Mission,* a novel based on his twenty-sixth mission. He did not know how fictionalized it was until he returned to the Czech Republic in 1994 to attend the rededication of a memorial to his crew in the village of Litice, outside of Pilzen. There he learned that his friend Mike Brennan had not died on the plane but had successfully bailed out. A German officer had killed him when he reached the ground.

College Years

When Mazer returned from the war, he, like many former soldiers, went to college on the GI Bill. In 1948, he received a bachelor of arts degree in history from Union College in Schenectady, New York. He says that the war had transformed the life of every kid from his neighborhood, hundreds of them. The GI Bill made money available for the education of World War II veterans, allowing them to go to college.

When Mazer first arrived home from the service, however, he wasn't sure he would go to college, and so he went to one of the many employment agencies in the city. On white cards posted outside buildings there were lists of entry-level positions and pay. Mazer found a job in a print shop, but he lasted less than one day. He had thought the work might lead to writing, but instead he was a delivery boy, expected to ride the subway to deliver packages throughout the city. Before his first day was half over, he sat on the subway thinking how foolish he was. He had available to him the 52-20 Plan, which would pay any World War II veteran $20 a week for a year; he need not work to receive the money. The delivery job paid the same. So, why work, when he could use the GI Bill to attend college and still get paid $20 per week? After he delivered the packages he'd been given that first morning, he never went back—never even returned to pick up his 2 hours' pay. Soon afterward, he enrolled in college.

Union College, which was all-male at the time, had been known as a big fraternity school, but it was transformed by the war. The college was full of returning GIs who were interested in things other than fraternities. Mazer enjoyed college but still did not have any plans for his life. He loved history and was interested in philosophy. He liked political economics and read Karl Marx, but he was terrible in the subject; he just couldn't understand it.

It was during his college years that he left the Jewish world completely behind him. He didn't tell anyone he was Jewish. He had worried about being Jewish during the war, when he decided to have an *H* for "Hebrew" shown on his dog tags. He was fearful of what trouble this might cause him if he was put in a prison camp, but he was lucky. The man who interrogated him after he was captured barely spoke English, and Mazer pretended not to understand German—although his knowledge of Yiddish allowed him to understand most of what was being said. He says that he feels sure that earlier in the war an *H* on a dog tag might have caused serious problems for prisoners, but cold, dumb, skin-of-the-teeth luck was with him.

While at Union College, Mazer had his antenna tuned to pick up anti-Semitic remarks, of which there were plenty. His main anxiety was whether he would respond properly to anti-Semitism. He had always been told he didn't look like a Jew, and he didn't announce it. But when remarks were made about Jews—"Jewing me down" or such remarks as "Jews are this, Jews are that . . ."— he had to respond.

Harry worked on the college newspaper and wrote stringers for the Schenectady *Gazette*. He found it very difficult work, although he was told by a teacher or two that "this was good stuff." During college he was writing other things as well, but he never took a writing course. He attempted to write fiction; he wrote mood pieces in which scenery was very important. To this day, the setting is central to the plots and character development of his books. He was not strongly attuned to story lines during these early years of writing. He had not yet learned how to plot: "It was hard—this is what I recall, how hard writing was" (interview with author).

Norma Fox

During college Harry Mazer first met Norma Fox. He saw her for the second time 2 years later, when she came to Schenectady to visit her sister during the 1948 presidential campaign for Henry Wallace, a third-party candidate who was running against Harry Truman. Mazer calls that campaign and their involvement in it— "that mad, incredible scene." They handed out and prepared literature for the campaign.

Following their second meeting, they began to date seriously. Norma was 17; Harry was 23. He was ready to get married, but she wanted to go to college. Nonetheless, they were married before the end of Norma's freshman year, on 12 February 1950.

The newlyweds lived in New York City for 4 months, but the heat, noise, and dirt troubled Norma, and so they moved back to Schenectady and lived in a two-family house with Norma's sister and brother-in-law. Anne, their first daughter, was born there in 1953, on either 1 April or 2 April. Mazer can never remember the exact date, since Gina, their fourth child, was born 10 years later on either 1 April or 2 April.

During these early years, neither of them looked at Mazer's work as merely labor—it was important political work. He was a union member and a welder. He had an ideological belief in the working class, in socialism. He saw his work in the factory, in union organizing, as a way to change the world. "I still had stars in my eyes about the working class. It was something we both accepted" (interview with author). But his politics and union organizing were not appreciated by the management in the plants where he worked, making it necessary for him to move the family from Schenectady to Passaic and then to Paterson, New Jersey, where Joseph was born in 1955; then back to Schenectady; and then to Utica, New York. In 1957 the family moved to Syracuse, where Susan was born.

By this time Mazer was losing his idealism. He was looking for something else—he didn't know what, but sheet-metal work and welding were not what he wanted. It was not merely that the job was less satisfying than it had been but that his ideology had changed: "I had had a great belief in socialism, a belief in the Soviet Union." But in 1955, after Stalin's atrocities were exposed for the first time, the Mazers discovered that the whole foundation of their politics was a lie: "Our ideals were not a lie, and our desire to make the world a better place wasn't a lie, but the real world was something else. I was just working, and it was like the lights faded. It went to reality, the leaden world I was in. It was deadening—life on the shop floor" (interview with author). The two of them had what he now laughingly calls a "seminal discussion": What was he to do with his life?

During those years, Norma Fox Mazer was working nights either as a waitress or in the market. They had two children, and they both needed to work. And then reality hit. At first, Harry thought he would go back to science, perhaps to become a chemist. He could see the importance of chemistry on his sheet-metal job. The men worked with copper, and there were terrible fumes. Ventilation was very important. They were continuously creating and rebuilding because the acid was rotting the metal of the ventilating systems. Mazer went to the office and said, "Give me a job in the lab." That was the beginning of a change, but nothing came of it. Then he thought he'd go into psychology—"that seemed interesting."

In 1957, Mazer was offered a job teaching history and English at Central Square High School. He taught tenth-grade English and tenth-grade world history. All together, he taught 150 students and had at least three classes to prepare. It was a heavy load, teaching and going to graduate school, but his wife helped him. He liked teaching; he had a good time, and he enjoyed the performance aspects of it: "I liked shocking these kids; I enjoyed that" (interview with author).

Although he liked teaching, Mazer taught for only 2 years. "My politics caught up with me," he says. These were the McCarthy years—years during which hearings were held in Schenectady, Syracuse, and other upstate New York cities—hearings to get the "radicals and reds out of the union. And people lost their jobs." Mazer doesn't know exactly how it happened, but someone went to the administration of the Central Square school district where he was teaching and told them that Harry Mazer was a communist—"which I wasn't." He believes it was someone in the American Legion who received information about his politics from the FBI. No matter how it happened, it was a difficult time. He had enjoyed teaching: "The high school principal liked me, and for a second-year teacher I was doing very well. I was dedicated, working hard. So he wouldn't have done anything, but with the politics of the time his hands were tied—he had no choice" (interview with author).

Becoming a Real Writer

Although this was a difficult time for Mazer, Norma saw the good in it. He couldn't write while he was teaching. So now he could go back to factory work and to writing. This marked the beginning of his career as a writer. In fact, this was the moment of their second "seminal discussion." They would both become writers.

> It wasn't just me. Norma wanted to write, too. If we didn't let ourselves get discouraged, didn't set ourselves impossible goals, if we wrote a little each day (fifteen minutes a day), then in time, maybe we would be writers. And that's the way we started, fifteen minutes a day.[10]

It was not easy. Norma was pregnant with their fourth child, and Harry was working all day: "We were writing two hours every morning before I went to work." They were beginning to produce things, and Harry wanted to get out of the factory—to make more time for writing: "We were devising schemes; we were always devising schemes." He smiles when he remembers one of these schemes to make more time for writing on the job: "As a pieceworker, you pace yourself. You don't want to work too fast, because the time-study man will come and time and re-time the operation and add more pieces to the day's work. You are careful to not finish your work in the morning, even though you could. You stretch the job out over the entire day." So, Mazer reports, "I was going to the john a lot. I always had a book in my back pocket. I remember I was reading Chekhov's short stories; I was analyzing them—trying to understand how the stories were put together. I was teaching myself—I was self-taught. I would sit in the john, and the foreman would come and knock at the door. 'What are you doing in there?'" (interview with author). Not surprisingly, supervisors were dissatisfied with Mazer. He would frequently take days off—working only 3 days a week—because he wanted to write. He and Norma had discovered that they could survive on 3 days' pay. They lived frugally, bought day-old bread, and paid $45 a month for rent. Harry was also fixing up the two-family house in which they lived with Norma's parents.

Finally, Harry quit his job. By that time, the Mazers had four young children. Then, because Norma had been injured in a car accident, they received a $1,500 settlement. Harry would quit his job. They figured they could live for 3 months on that money. They'd use that time to see whether they could support themselves writing.

Initially both the Mazers wrote for pulp magazines. Harry's first article as a professional writer was a historical essay called "Boatload of Brides," which appeared in *Adventure* magazine. It was about women textile workers in New England who became known as Mercer's Maids, since the imaginative man who devised the scheme was named Mercer. Harry's article told the story of how these women, during a period of unemployment, volunteered to make the long boat trip around the Straits of Magellan to Seattle and nearby territories to become wives of the men there who had no women. These were adventurous women.

Like the women about whom he had written, Mazer, too, was adventurous—willing to live on almost nothing to realize his dream of becoming a writer. For "Boatload of Brides" he was paid about $300. That gave the Mazers another month to keep writing. Norma, at that time, was writing anecdotes for children's magazines and "confession" stories for which she was paid 2 or 3 cents a word. Harry tried his hand at this kind of writing. He remembers his first story, "The Garden of Roses." It is about a man who has a couple of daughters and believes his wife is going to have a son. When she has another daughter, he is depressed and acts badly. This story was written shortly after Gina, their youngest daughter, was born, and Mazer admits to behaving badly: "We dealt with it. Norma recognized something was wrong immediately. It didn't last long" (interview with author). From this story Mazer was learning how to turn his own world—the events of his life—into fiction.

The Mazers began to realize that they could make a living writing. It was hard. They each had to turn out a 5,000-word story every week. According to Mazer, "You needed more than one idea; you needed three ideas to get one idea that would be viable. And you had to talk the idea" (interview with author). This may have been the beginning of their writing partnership, a collaboration that has resulted in three jointly written young adult novels.

Developing characters for their stories was the least difficult part, remembers Mazer. "Confession" writers focus on misguided people who have abnormal relationships and feel pain. Coming up with the story itself was more difficult. But the conclusions were relatively easy, because in confessions the character must be redeemed. These confession stories supported the Mazers for several years and in many ways provided a strong foundation for the novels they would later write separately and together. Writing confessions taught them the importance of solid ideas, structure, and constant rewriting. Writing was hard work.

As a young man Harry Mazer, like many young writers, assumed that writing was largely inspiration. He had to learn to sit in one place and to be patient. He learned that he might have to write a hundred words to get the right one (Illinois Librarians). It was writing these pulp stories, reading, and recognizing that many great writers (Hemingway, Steinbeck, Erskine Caldwell) had begun their careers writing pulp fiction that kept the Mazers writing. Finally, each of them was ready to write a book.

Norma laughs when she remembers that she would tell Harry: "Not me before you, honey. I actually told him I wouldn't publish a book before him. I was protecting his male ego." But Norma's first novel, *I, Trissy,* and Harry's first novel, *Guy Lenny,* were published at exactly the same moment. The year was 1971, and Harry Mazer's career as a writer of good literature for young adults was launched.

2. Coming of Age: Separation

Harry Mazer's books examine the coming of age of adolescent males. Each of his books looks at the development—education in its broadest sense—of a younger or older adolescent. This is particularly true of four of his books: *The War on Villa Street, The Girl of his Dreams, The Dollar Man,* and *I Love You, Stupid!* The first two examine the same adolescent protagonist (Willis Pierce) as he grows from an intense, lonely preadolescent to a 19-year-old who is on his own, having run away from home at 18. The second two deal with Marcus Rosenbloom, who, like Willis, has a secret life in which he first dreams of the father he never knew and later dreams of the sex life he will have. Both Willis and Marcus grow physically and emotionally. As Tobi Tobias says about *The Dollar Man* in the *New York Times Book Review,* it is the "charged energy" of Mazer's work and the authenticity of his characters that make us care, very much, what happens to them.[1]

Mazer recognizes that the protagonists' authenticity occurs because each has his own voice—a voice that he has heard clearly and internalized, a voice from his own life. Mazer claims that both Willis and Marcus possess traits of people he has known well. He talks of Marcus as the one protagonist from all of his books who, although completely fictional, is most like him. (The other protagonist who is obviously Mazer is Jack Raab in *The Last Mission,* a book that might be classified as autobiographical fiction.) Marcus, like Mazer, has an active inner life or imagination and is in search of the father he has never known. He is a dreamer who poses as a writer.

Willis, on the other hand, is the opposite of Mazer. "Willis is everything I wasn't. . . . Willis is tight. He's physical. He's fast. He's an athlete. He's a runner. Emotionally, he's like my father" (interview with author).

Stages of Rites of Passage

In primitive societies the rite of passage was often a ritual, which still exists in a few modern religious and cultural events. The anthropologist Arnold van Gennep has described the rite of passage as having three phases: *separation, margin,* and *aggregation.*

According to van Gennep, during the *separation* stage young men, either alone or in a group of their peers, were separated from the community. This is certainly true of both of Mazer's protagonists as early adolescents. Marcus (*The Dollar Man*) is fat and has only one true friend. In spite of the advice of his friend, he attempts to become part of a troubled crowd who eventually cause him to be falsely accused of smoking dope in school. He fantasizes continually about the father he has never known. According to one review of the novel, "Marcus is looking for his father everywhere: in Dorrity, the leader of a delinquent, teen-age gang that reluctantly befriends him and, predictably, betrays him; in Bill, his mother's long-time friend and lover; in authorities of school and the law whose obtuse, almost cynical, callousness to the young is appalling here; and in heroic fantasies like the one of a mythic 'dollar man' who generously 'gives where there is 'need.'"[2]

During the separation stage, it is not unusual in real life or in novels for peers to take center stage while parents are noticeably absent. Willis's father (*The War on Villa Street*) is an alcoholic who continually embarrasses his son, so much so that Willis chooses to have no friends. "Every moment in his life his [Willis's] father is on his mind, leaning on him, getting to him, abusing him. It is almost more than eighth-grader Willis Pierce can bear; an alcoholic father with a thick, French-Canadian accent and a menial factory job."[3]

Like many boys in early adolescence, Marcus and Willis have better, though at times distant, relationships with their mothers. Marcus only knows Sally, his mother, and thinks of her as a friend at the same time as he resents her for not revealing any information about his father. "Sally is unmarried, charmingly forthright in personal style, and stubbornly self-sufficient, but she gives Marcus nothing of his father—not a picture, not a name."[4] Willis helps his mother deal with her alcoholic husband, even going to collect his paycheck before he can spend it on drink.

During the *margin* stage in primitive societies, boys remained apart while the actual rite was performed. This often required the boy to complete a task needed in order for the tribe or family to survive. For example, the boy might hunt and kill an animal for food. As in the separation stage, the boys were often left on their own to fend for themselves. This isolation was and is necessary because whether in primitive or contemporary society, little growth takes place when an adolescent is controlled or directed by someone other than himself.

Mazer recognizes the need to remove the adolescent from parents and peers so that growth can occur. In each of his books peers become antagonists, and frequently the protagonist's task is to deal with this antagonism in a way that promotes maturity. In *The Dollar Man,* Marcus wants to have friends, even those who do not represent the values of his family. However, he is frequently tormented by the boys and ridiculed by the girls. "Marcus Rosenbloom is fat and he daydreams. He has a large fantasy life and a large rubber tire of fat around his gut. Both seem to be the result of an understandable, greedy emotional hunger—the acute longing of adolescence—for love, identity, communication, roots."[5] Willis Pierce appears as a secondary character in *The Dollar Man* as one of Marcus's primary tormentors, calling him "Rosen Balloon":

> Marcus hates Willis, and for good reason. In school whenever the teacher left the room, the other students would practically fall off their seats laughing as Willis waddled around imitating Marcus. . . . "Clump, clump, clump, this is the way you look, Rosen Balloon," Willis would huff, slapping his feet down heav-

ily on the floor. "Everyone head for the hills! Here comes Marcus the Elephant!"[6]

Although Marcus hates Willis in *The Dollar Man,* Willis later becomes the sympathetic protagonist of *The War on Villa Street.* Mazer explains how the intersection between the two novels occurred:

> In *The Dollar Man* there's nothing likeable about Willis Pierce; I didn't like him, myself. Toward the end of *The Dollar Man* there's a scene where Marcus, standing on the roof of an apartment house, looks down into the lighted windows of another building. Marcus, who hungers for the love of the father he's never known sees Willis and his father sitting at a table across from each other. When I began to think about the story that became *The War on Villa Street* that rooftop scene came back to me. I kept thinking about it, coming back to it. Maybe it was what Marcus thought that interested me: "He was seeing Willis in a secret way, a way he wasn't supposed to, but one that was more truthful than all the other ways."[7]

Mazer says that he often creates characters whom he intensely dislikes, perhaps because he recognizes that his protagonists must learn to respond to these people in ways that promote personal growth. But then, he admits, that he finds these characters fascinating. He wants to know why they are so unlikable. He wants to watch as they confront their own internal and external enemies.

This phenomenon began with his first book, *Guy Lenny.* Mazer created a character named Tony LaPorte. We don't know much about him—he appears on only 2 pages. However, we do recognize that he is not a very sympathetic character—that his major interest, according to Mazer, is "making smart-ass remarks about the girls. I didn't like him much." For some reason, Mazer became interested in Tony, and Tony later became the protagonist of *Snow Bound.* Mazer reflects that the idea for the book came before the characters, so he had to think of who would be in it. He deliberately picked Tony LaPorte because he was not likable. In the beginning of *Snow Bound* there is nothing endearing about Tony. According to Mazer, Tony was a part of the dynamic of the book and made it work: "He wasn't particularly good, kind, or thoughtful. There was nothing redeeming about him." Tony must overcome these detestable characteristics if he is to mature and survive. So, originally Tony was created by Mazer to provide an opportunity for Guy to confront evil, but Mazer's interest in why and how Tony became so mean made him an excellent protagonist for a survival novel in which maturity is required to overcome the environment.

This was also true of Willis's creation. He first appears in *The Dollar Man* as Marcus's enemy. Mazer reflects, "I needed somebody in the book to torment him, the way I used to be tormented because I was a fat kid" (interview with author). Willis becomes a part of the fabric of the book. He forces Marcus to grow as a human being as he begins to realize that Willis too has problems, that he is not as strong or as evil as he seems.

Willis then became the protagonist of *The War on Villa Street*. Like Marcus, he too is tormented. In his case, his tormentors are a gang of young men who vow to destroy him when he refuses to allow them to have a meeting in his apartment. He, like Marcus, is ridiculed by girls and is made fun of for his "friendship" with Richard, a 16-year-old retarded boy. But it is more than this that separates Willis from his peers. "Willis knew, knew it in his bones. It was his father's drinking, the drinking and the funny way he talked that made him, Willis, an outsider."[8] Mazer reflects that the characters he dislikes have a reason for being so unlikable. It is these reasons—these problems in their lives—that make them interesting people to write about, that give them authenticity and voice. Likewise, it is these problems that isolate them and allow them to grow. Mazer says of Willis Pierce, "I got to love the character" (interview with author).

According to Arnold van Gennep, if the boys of primitive societies successfully met the requirements of the rite or task performed during the margin stage of passage, they moved to the *aggregation* stage, in which they became fully participating members of adult society. Often a celebration or ceremony occurred to mark their new status. In the sequels to both books, Marcus and Willis begin to move into adult society.

Willis learns in *The Girl of His Dreams* that his dream girl may be the girl he has rejected and that he can share his passion for running with others. Marcus, too, struggles to enter adult society, which he thinks of as crossing "the wall," the wall between childhood and adulthood which can be crossed only by two people together. He tells his friend Wendy: "It's like the Great Wall of China, only this wall is bigger and longer and goes all around the world. It divides the whole human race. Every human being is either on one side of the wall or the other."⁹ In Marcus's immature thinking, the only way to become an adult is by having sexual intercourse. Marcus believes that if Wendy agrees to have sex with him, they will both be adults. And, for a while, after they make a pact to help each other over the wall, they do feel like adults: "Racing along with the cars, he felt comradely, friendly, a man among men. Yesterday he'd been a kid with his tongue hanging out, but today, today, I am a man!" (*Stupid,* 146). Wendy, too, believes that their newly found sexual relationship makes them more mature, but unlike Marcus she is not so sure she likes the responsibility:

> "I thought I would feel good. You know, it's over with, I did it, hooray, and all that. But—" She linked arms with him. "I keep getting these weird, possessive thoughts. Like, He's mine, mine, mine!"
> He smiled, "It's all right with me."
> "Not with me. I don't want to own anyone. Just because we— No, I really didn't think it would be this way." (*Stupid,* 147–48)

Neither Marcus nor Willis is able to enter adult society on his own; it is now that they each must move from being separated to becoming a part of and accepting responsibility for the feelings of others. In both books, the girls have more intense and mature feelings for the boys than the boys have for them. In *The Girl of His Dreams* "the initial inequality of [Willis's and Sophie's] feelings is what gives the book its earliest and most dramatic tension."¹⁰ However, the book emphasizes the "conflicts and tenderness [of their growing relationship], with emphasis on Sophie's strength. She's willing to love but not settle for less than equality."¹¹

It is Wendy in *I Love You, Stupid!* who helps Marcus see that until he acknowledges the feelings of others, he will not cross the wall into adulthood. Wendy tells Marcus when they break up, "Sex is not a good enough reason for sex" (167). Marcus doesn't get it, but Wendy calls the sexual relationship off. As the days go by, Marcus begins to realize that he misses Wendy for reasons other than sex. She is the one he wants to tell when he has an offer to have one of his stories published. At one point, Marcus writes in an unmailed letter to Wendy, "How can I make you believe me? How can I prove that I mean what I say? I liked us!" (174).

Although an actual ceremony marking the young male's acceptance into adult society is not as common today, certainly not to the extent it was in more primitive societies, it can still be observed in some religious customs such as bar mitzvah, which in Judaism marks the boy's arrival at the age of responsibility. The bar mitzvah, the ceremony celebrating this event, follows the boy's study in Hebrew of the Torah, the body of Jewish religious literature. Confirmation in the Roman Catholic Church and in many Protestant churches, and believers' baptism in several Christian faiths, also mark the attainment of religious responsibility and are celebrated by a ritual. Because these ceremonies acknowledge the young person's newfound maturity, they require adult mentorship and participation.

Nonreligious society also has some ceremonial rites of passage. A few are proceeded, in a less formal sense, by a test of the adolescent's adult capabilities. Some of these events, such as high school graduation, require individual preparation and testing. However, contemporary adolescents are rarely expected to complete formal tasks or rites proving their capability to enter and contribute to society. Many events that require adolescents to pass tests have no formal ceremony but do remove the young from adult society. Such things as going away to college, going to camp, entering the military, or even getting a driver's license might fall into this category.

In contemporary society, markers of maturation need not involve a rite or celebration, and vice versa. A prom is an example of a celebration which is not really a marker, and acceptance by a college is an example of a marker without formal ceremony. In fact, many young people rebel against participation in events designed to acknowledge their accomplishments and maturity, as both Marcus and Willis do. Rebellion against adults has itself become a kind of rite and ceremony of passage and is a hallmark of modern adolescence. Some young people seek independence—separation from society—within religions that differ from their parents. Others search for it in social or sexual rebellion. Some run away; some seek the ultimate separation—suicide. Neither Marcus nor Willis ever considers going to this extreme; but Marcus, who has always been close to his mother, finds himself increasingly in conflict with her. At one point, when he tells his mother he wants to quit school to become a writer, she tries to persuade him to compromise—to go to school part of the day, completing his graduation requirements, and to use the rest of the day to write:

> "I'm going to write every day," he said. "Every day, all day."
> "Write all day? Be realistic," Sally said. "It's impossible for you to sit still for thirty seconds." (*Stupid,* 53)

Even after Marcus agrees to stay in school and graduate, he does not want to participate in his own graduation ceremony and does so only because his mother insists on it.

In contemporary society the ceremonies marking the successful completion of a passage are sometimes formal, but more often they are informal. For all of Mazer's characters, separation from their families is the rite of passage—the test for his adolescent protagonists. For some this route toward independence is chosen for them (by the divorce or death of parents, for example); others select this road to maturity without the knowledge of their parents (by running away); and some of them merely separate themselves from their parents while still living at home. However, all of his protagonists to a lesser or greater extent are growing up on their own. For Mazer's protagonists, as for most contemporary adolescents, there is no formal ceremony to mark their successful passage. It is for them to determine when they are ready to take on the responsibilities of adulthood. In all of Mazer's novels, the characters grow and mature, but a reader is never sure whether they are entirely ready to accept the challenges and responsibilities of adulthood.

3. Coming of Age: Connections

Connecting with Parents

"KILL OFF PARENTS." According to Harry Mazer, "Parents are always a problem in a book, especially when you're writing about young protagonists who you hope will be brave and resourceful and solve their own problems."[1] Mazer takes his own advice in all of his novels. In each of them, one and often both of the protagonist's parents are missing. They have deserted their children, or have died, or are simply out of the picture. Mazer's books are not unique in this. Many young adult coming-of-age books have absent parents. More often than not, when the protagonist is female, the mother is absent; and when the protagonist is male, the father is absent. Even when parents are present in coming-of-age books, the protagonist usually distances herself or himself from them. Of course, this is necessary—as it is in life—if the protagonist is to grow into a mature and responsible adult.

Many adult readers of young adult books have criticized their authors for the limited role of parents in the lives of the protagonists. Some critics contend that the absence of parents makes the books unrealistic. Others suggest that the absence of parents makes the protagonists in the novels poor models for young adults. However, author after author has defended the absence of parents as a necessary conceit for books in which adolescents grow into adulthood. In fact, in many young adult novels, including some of Mazer's books, the maturing process of the adolescent includes learning to accept his or her parents as human beings with faults, as Willis does in *The Girl of His Dreams,* just as the parents learn to accept the adolescent as an individual who must take and assume responsibility.

For example, Sally—Marcus's mother in *I Love You, Stupid!*—is beginning to learn that she can no longer protect Marcus from people who might hurt him; nor can she protect him from mistakes he might make. She must begin to treat him as an adult who takes responsibility and accepts responsibility for himself and for others. Although the novel is the story of the unlikely romance of Marcus and Wendy and "I love you, stupid!" is what Marcus says to Wendy at the end of the book, it might be something that Sally mutters under her breath to her son. When Marcus decides to quit school to write full time, it is Sally who comes up with a successful compromise that gives Marcus the opportunity to practice his writing but also keeps him in school until graduation:

> "All right, let's talk seriously," she said later, "see if we can work out something." Why couldn't they meet halfway, she said. Compromise. She was willing to give, so he should be, too. "For instance, why don't you rearrange your schedule. Drop the courses you don't need, keep the ones you do need. Can't you take the classes you need in the morning, say, then have your afternoons free for writing?"
>
> Halfway measures: that was Sally. But in a way he was relieved. She was satisfied, and for the time being so was he. (*Stupid,* 55)

For parents and for adolescents, this transition from dependence and unconditional love to independence and respect is rarely easy.

Connecting with Our Inner Lives

It is also true in Mazer's novels that the adolescent protagonist is frequently removed from siblings and peers. The phenomenon of the adolescent alone as a literary technique of initiation novels was discussed in Chapter 2. However, in Mazer's books it appears that the loneliness of the adolescent is more than a literary technique that allows the author to develop the adolescent character. In Mazer's books, the adolescent is almost always alone. This may be because Harry Mazer as an adolescent was often alone. The aloneness of his characters may also stem from his belief that it is "the inner life that connects us all."[2] According to Mazer, it is the inner life that makes it possible for an adult to write for an adolescent audience.

When Mazer writes of his own adolescence, he often talks about being alone. Although young Harry had many friends and was active with them at the Bronx High School of Science and in the community of the co-ops, it was his inner life—the books he read and his posing as a writer—that shaped his world. Harry frequently visited the public library, and as a child he read when there were few books in his home. He "dreamed of making the world a better place."[3] It is our inner lives, according to Mazer, that causes each of us to be unique and alone in our own dreams and fantasies, distorted realities, hopes, and disappointments. However, it is the common pain and joy we share in our inner lives that join us one to the other.

Mazer reveals that one of his first attempts at writing dealt with his shattered dreams of Isabel, the sixth-grade fantasy romance of his own life, and of Marcus's life in *I Love You, Stupid!* He admits that he can't ever remember having a relationship with a girl or having any friends who were girls. He recalls instead that his relationships with girls were in the books he read. Girls were a part of his active inner life. Marcus—and young Harry Mazer—share the frustration of thwarted nonrelationships and the desire to write. Marcus is a budding writer, and one of his first successful attempts at writing is a piece about his fantasy and the ultimate humiliation caused when a young girl, Vivian, rejects him. Mazer's Vivian was Isabel, a girl in his "sixth-grade class in PS 96 in the Bronx, a tall, skinny girl with long hair."

Mazer also reveals that he was a lot like the younger Marcus in *The Dollar Man.* Mazer's sixth-grade class picture shows him to be "a big fat kid, in need of a haircut, the only one wearing a dark shirt in a field of white shirts and blouse." Mazer, like the

younger Marcus, longed to be a part of the crowd, but he was
alone in his fantasy world:

> I never spoke to Isabel. I never talked to anyone about her. Not
> my friends, certainly not my parents. I followed her around
> everywhere. She lived on the third floor of an apartment house
> on Bronx Park East. In the evening after supper, I used to stand
> across the street from her house and look longingly up at the
> lighted windows and wonder which one was hers.
>
> Once I boldly crossed the street, and went up the stairs, and
> stood outside her door. What was I doing there? What did I
> want? What would I have done if she had opened the door? What
> if it was her father? The moment I heard a noise at the door I
> fled.
>
> She noticed me only once. I was across the street one day.
> She was with a girl friend. When they saw me they threw their
> arms around each other and started laughing and jeering at me.[4]

In *The Dollar Man,* Marcus is only slightly older than Mazer
was when he met Isabel, and Marcus also stands out on the street
looking longingly up at Vivian's windows, dreaming of rescuing
her from an imagined foe while he fantasizes about the father he
has never known. Like the author as a young man, his characters
have inner lives that place them in a fantasy world where they are
never truly alone, where they have fathers who love them and
friends who never betray them, and where they are worshiped by
the most beautiful girls in the school. And, like the author's inner
world of fantasy, these worlds remove the characters from the
real world of fathers who are absent from their lives, peers who
betray them, and beautiful girls who humiliate them. They are
alone to find their way into the frightening world of adulthood—
the world beyond the "wall" that Marcus suggests separates
childhood dreams from adult reality.

Although Harry Mazer now has a large family and a loving wife,
he has maintained an active inner world. He still shares the inner
life of the young through his own experiences and through the
stories he creates. According to Mazer, "the emotions of the
young are not a foreign country. We've all been there. We recognize our ties to the young, even when they don't recognize their

ties to us." He suggests that the problems which the young face may change, "but the underlying emotions remain the same."[5] In an interview in *Contemporary Authors,* Mazer talks about his aloneness as a writer dwelling in a world of feelings:

> I think really what informs my writing and keeps me in this field is an interest in the secret parts of a character, not what people say and do so much as what they think and feel: the areas where they feel deprived, their longings, their feelings of separation, isolation. Much more than anything else I write out of a memory of those feelings.
>
> There are some writers who say they remember everything. I would hardly say that; I think I've *forgotten* everything. I've certainly forgotten the details. But I think I know the feelings, and that's what I really write out of.[6]

The aloneness of the adolescent in Mazer's books is more than a technique that allows the adolescent to grow; it is also an exploration of the author's inner world of feelings. Through his characters, Mazer explores the fantasy world of his own adolescence. In becoming his characters, he is able to examine this inner world from the perspective of an adult. And, because these feelings and frustrations remain the same for each new generation of adolescents, Mazer's own world and the inner world of his characters connect his books and him to his readers.

However, in Mazer's books, as in his own life, his characters do not reach adulthood entirely on their own. It is only through the connections of their inner lives with the realities of their real worlds that they grow into independent, responsible adults who care as much about the feeling of others as they care about themselves.

Connections with Mentors

Young Mazer's friendship with Joe Keen helped convince him of the importance of mentors in the lives of the young. Keen was entirely different from Mazer's parents, but, nonetheless, he was a family friend who was an acceptable mentor for their impressionable young son. Harry and Joe did many things together, and when Mazer was 16, he worked for Keen doing different kinds of summer jobs.

The role of crucial adults in the lives of adolescents adds to the moral fiber of Mazer's works. Those who criticize the adult characterization in his novels as "pretty skimpy,"[7] miss the point. Although the adults may be missing in their immediate families as the adolescents struggle for their own independence, it is through the involvement of other adults and more mature teenagers that the young characters grow.

In *When the Phone Rang*, Kevin does not become a responsible adult the minute he learns of his parents' death in a plane crash. He is not ready to take responsibility for his younger brothers and sisters, although they believe that only he can help them stay together. Kevin doesn't want to cook, clean the house, or make the younger Keller children attend school. He wants to return to the normal life of a college student. However, through the help of Uncle Paul and Grandma Betty—who recognize the children's need to remain a family—Kevin begins to understand how he can be responsible for himself and for his siblings. This new understanding and strength do not occur alone, however, but are symbolized at the end of the novel, when Kevin removes his father's cowboy hat—which he has been wearing throughout most of the book—throws it into the river, and watches it sink. Kevin is ready to accept the responsibilities of adulthood on his own.

Connections with Life's Harsh Realities

In many of Mazer's novels, the entry into adulthood comes after confronting and overcoming a hostile environment. This, too, is drawn from the experiences of Mazer's life. Like Jack Raab in *The Last Mission,* Mazer joined the Army Air Corps as a young man of 17. Although Mazer was older than Jack, who is only 15, he, too, wanted to fight the Germans. Like Jack, he was a Jewish boy from the Bronx with fantasies of heroism, conquest, and finding out what it means to be a real man:

In 1943 I was 17 years old and so eager to get into the Army and into the war against Hitler that I volunteered for the Air Force and then had to beg my mother to sign the papers. It was a war we all believed in. We were Jews, and we hated Hitler and Fascism. It was the best of all possible wars, a war of righteousness, of good against evil, of right against wrong.[8]

Like Jack, Mazer learned that war is not heroes and glory. He says in "Two Boys from the Bronx," an unpublished essay, that the reality of war was "something else." Jack's distaste for fighting grows; with each boring mission he is more afraid. He worries about his family and dreams of seeing them again. When he is the only surviving member of the crew after its twenty-sixth mission is shot down over Czechoslovakia, Jack is captured by the Germans and witnesses the confusion of their defeat. He returns home, not as the conquering hero of his dreams but as a young man who has witnessed the horrors of war, survived, and will never be the same. However, it is not until he faces the parents of his best friend, Chuckie, who was killed on the mission, and hears himself telling his high school classmates the truth about war that Jack and the readers realize that he is becoming a responsible adult. Jack is not sure what he will say to his classmates until he stands before them, but once he begins, the words give new meaning to his experiences:

My name is Jack Raab. . . . I was in the Eighth Air Force. I'm a Jew. I wanted to fight Hitler. I got in the Air Corps by lying about my real age. . . . I'm glad I served. . . . I'm glad we won . . . . We couldn't let Hitler keep going. We had to stop him. But, most of all, I'm glad it's over. . . . I don't like war. I thought I'd like it before. But war is stupid. War is one stupid thing after another. I saw my best friend killed. His name was Chuckie O'Brien. My whole crew was killed. . . . A lot of people were killed. Millions of people. Ordinary people. Not only by Hitler. Not only on our side. War isn't like the movies. It's not fun and songs. It's not about heroes. It's about awful, sad things, like my friend Chuckie that I'm never going to see again. . . . I hope war never happens again. . . . That's all I've got to say.[9]

Mazer, like Jack, experienced the disappointment of unrealized heroism and the horrors of war:

> My dreams of being an officer, a pilot, were never realized. Instead I became a waist gunner. Almost as good. Now I dreamed of shooting down Nazi planes. I flew 26 missions in Europe and never got to do any brave or heroic deed. I never once fired my gun. I was scared every time we flew. . . . On our 26th mission we flew over Pilzen, Czechoslovakia, to bomb the Skoda Munitions Works. We missed our target, turned over the target again, and were hit. I saw Mike, who was our radio operator, frozen in the door of the radio room. He never made it out of the plane. Only three of us parachuted. Two of the three survived. No one in the plane lived. (*ALAN Review*, 1)

As Jack's thoughts suggest in the last paragraph of *The Last Mission*—perhaps prophetically, Mazer now maintains—the war does not end even when it is over: "He sat down. He hardly heard the applause. The floor of the radio room was still slippery with Chuckie's blood. . . . Dave was still fumbling with his chute . . . the plane was still falling through the sky" (*Mission*, 188).

Mazer's war has not ended either. In 1994, he had the opportunity to speak at the rededication of a monument to the men of his crew who were shot down and killed near Pilzen. At first he didn't want to go, but the only other survivor of his crew, Bill O'Malley, could not go. And, although he believed the war was behind him, he felt that he had to go so that he would not abandon again his best friend, Mike Brennan, who he believed had crashed with the plane. For nearly 50 years, Mazer had wondered whether he had abandoned Mike when he jumped backward from the crippled plane and left him standing, as Jack left Chuckie standing, with a frozen look on his face. It was not until he returned to what is now the Czech Republic, to the little town of Litice, and met Mirek Kahout, a young Czech who worked in the plant they had bombed and who had been researching the crash of Mazer's plane and death of his crew, that he learned the truth. Mazer had not abandoned Mike. Mike had bailed out of the plane but had been executed by a German Wehrmacht officer shortly after he hit the ground. He was buried with the rest of the crew in an unmarked, common grave, the only one with a bullet wound.

While Mazer spoke slowly in English, which was translated simultaneously into Czech, he came to understand why he had come, and he realized that his war has not ended:

> When I spoke, I said the names of each of my crew members, where they came from, and how old they were when they died. I had come back, uncertain what I was doing, maybe searching for a way to talk again to Mike. I wasn't having complicated thoughts about life and death. I was moved just saying Mike's name, the names of my crew, and I had to speak slowly to keep my voice steady. ("Two Boys," 8)

Jack in *The Last Mission* grows up when his inner world intersects with the real world. And—even though Mazer admits that when he wrote the last paragraph of the novel, he did not recognize that he was saying that his war had not ended when it was over—it is Jack's thoughts that lead to our knowledge that he will grow into a mature adult able to accept what Mazer now recognizes. "When we went off to war we were young. We had little sense of life except that it was ours, and so was fortune and possibility. I didn't know then, I couldn't have known what I know now-the cold dumb, skin-of-the-teeth luck that life is" ("Two Boys," 9).

Connections with Girls

Although teenagers rarely mature when group mentality is dictating their behavior, the intervention of others in the adolescent's inner world is required for growth to occur. Teenagers who remain completely isolated can become insular, removed from the real world. In several of Mazer's novels, as in his own life, this intervention comes from a meaningful relationship with a girl. As noted earlier, Harry met Norma Fox when she was only 15 and he was 21. He was a student at Union College in Schenectady after having served in World War II. Mazer remembers that meeting even though they did not see each other again for 2 years. He says that even at that early age Norma was beautiful and smart and a writer. When they met again 2 years later, in 1948, both Harry's and Norma's older sisters were involved in a political campaign for the Progressive party's presidential candidate. Harry had graduated from college and was working. Norma was still in high school. Although he thought Norma was too young for him, it was not long after she entered Antioch College as a freshman that she returned home to marry him. He was 24, and she was 18.

Norma's entry into Harry's life—her intelligence, her dream of becoming a writer, and her practical nature—helped him see that it might be possible, if he wrote each day and little by little learned how to write, to realize his own dream. Mazer admits that it was not easy. He has never found writing easy and does not think of himself as a natural writer. "I write and speak with difficulty," he says. "I am a writer not because this is something I do well—an inborn talent—but perhaps for the opposite reason, because I do it so poorly."[10] By contrast, "Norma wrote more easily, and she produced many more images and words, and she had lovely facility of language. My tendency has always been to try to shape it in my head before I dare say this word for which I'll be ridiculed, before I say something I'll be ashamed of" (interview with author).

From the beginning, Mazer had to work very hard, and Norma kept him on task. While Norma was pregnant with their fourth child, she woke up at 3:30 each morning. She convinced Harry that while the other children slept and before he went to work was a good time to write. So, each morning from about 3:30 until about 6:00 or 6:30 the Mazers would go to their desks on a converted back porch and write. Harry says that he could not have found the discipline to write this regularly if Norma was not keeping the same schedule.

It is probably because of the mutually supportive and loving relationship that Norma and Harry have shared for over four decades that Mazer appreciates and understands the role a young woman can play in the life and dreams of a young man. He focuses on the development of maturing relationships in his books *I Love You, Stupid!*, *Hey, Kid! Does She Love Me?*, and *The Girl of His Dreams*. In each of these novels, the adolescent male protagonist is a young man who lives in an inner dream world. Each is trying to find himself, and each is searching for the perfect girl—not for the perfect relationship. None of these young men recognizes the importance of the development of a mutually supportive relationship at the start of the novels, but the female protagonists help them discover who they really are—beyond their superficial images of themselves as a runner, a writer, and a movie director. Each of these young men thinks of a relationship in terms of what it does for him, primarily concerning sex but also how the girl reflects on what others think of him. It is only through their growing friendships with strong female protagonists that they learn that image has no part in meaningful relationships and that sex is only one part of how men and women support and love each other. It is through the sharing of their inner worlds with another person that the characters grow toward adulthood.

Connecting with Ourselves

In ourselves we find the strength we need to control our own lives, to move from dreams to reality. Cleo, in *The Island Keeper,* must learn to care more about herself, to believe in herself. If she does not, she will not survive. When she runs away from her father and grandmother after the tragic death of her sister Jam, Cleo flees a life in which she feels unloved and blames herself for her problems, even those over which she has no control. She escapes to the island she remembers from the happier days of her youth. But now she is alone. She thinks she has prepared herself for her adventure by purchasing food supplies and camping gear, but she has no idea how quickly the food will be gone and she will be forced to find ways to feed herself. She also does not recognize the problems she will encounter with no shelter: animals, weather, insects, terror. She must find a way to protect herself from the environment she has chosen.

Cleo believes that she can always leave the island in the canoe that brought her to it safely. But she has been on the island only in the summer. She does not recognize the potential hazards of Canadian storms. When the canoe is destroyed, her escape route is gone. She must now survive entirely by her wits and her strength. Cleo has never thought of herself as either intelligent or strong. She thinks of herself as fat, weak, and controlled by a grandmother and father who would prefer to have her out of their lives. Now her only choice is either to learn how to survive—by finding and storing food, hunting animals for food and skins, and creating shelter and warmth—or to die. Her experiences on the island and her eventual escape by crossing the frozen lake convince her that she alone is in control of her life. At the end of the novel, Cleo agrees to return to St. Ives, her boarding school, and recognizes that she is no longer the same person and is no longer alone because she has the strength she has found on the island:

> She hadn't forgotten the way she'd been at St. Ives before, in a dream most of the time, only coming alive on vacations when she was with Jam. She didn't want to go back to being like that. She didn't have to. Things had happened—the island had happened. The island . . . the island. . . .
> She remembered the first time she saw the deer in the inlet and discovered the stream and how the island opened before her. All that movement around her, the swimming creatures, the air vibrating with the hum of insects and birds, the life on the hills and in the water. It was still there, under the snow. She would go back. She closed her eyes, invoked the strength of the island, drew it close around her.[11]

Mazer's books let readers know that they are alone only if they choose to remain alone. Even if there is no other person to love or to be loved by, we can find inner strength that allows us to move from our dream worlds into a reality we create and control.

Tolley learns this in *Cave under the City.* Unlike Cleo, he finds his strength not by surviving on an island but by surviving in a big city during the Great Depression. Although in many ways he must struggle alone, he has someone to love and someone who depends on him. Bubber, his 5-year-old brother, relies on Tolley for nearly everything—for food, for shelter, for medicine, for attention, and for love. By caring about and for someone else, Tolley learns to care more about and for himself.

The relationship between Tolley and Bubber and their attempt to survive on their own in the city by hiding in a cellar of a burned-out restaurant also intersects with Mazer's life. The cellar was a place where Harry played in his youth. The dumbwaiter was there, and so was the burned-out shell of a building. The apartments that Mazer describes in the novel are the co-ops, the project in which he spent his youth, and he also had a younger brother. Like Bubber, his brother was not as capable as he and was frequently in trouble. Mazer remembers that his brother did very badly in school; his father says that he caught him drinking at 9. However, in the book it is Bubber, in spite of the fact that he cannot read, who helps Tolley realize that they must return home, that they can confront the dangers there better than they can on the streets.

Eddie, in *Who Is Eddie Leonard?* must also learn to love and care for himself. Eddie is an orphan who has lived with his grandmother since he was a young boy. He is never sure how he came to be with her. At various times she tells him that his mother (her daughter) abandoned him at birth. At other times she tells him that he was found in a garbage can or on a park bench. Eddie and his grandmother are poor, but they manage to survive. She is old, sick, and sometimes irrational. Eddie is frequently left alone.

When Eddie is 14, his grandmother is hospitalized, and he is left alone for a long time. Although she had never been much of a mother, when she dies Eddie realizes that he is really all alone:

> I went down the stairs, and out on the street. There was something inside me, something tight, that wanted to break out. Something hard that wouldn't let go. It wasn't my grandmother. It wasn't that. I didn't feel a lot, no tears, there was no catch in my throat. No, what I felt, that hard thing, was fear. *You're alone,* it said. *You said you were alone. Now you really are, and you can't stand it.*[12]

One day Eddie sees a poster of a missing boy, Jason Diaz. The more he looks at the poster and compares it with himself in the mirror, the more he is sure that *he* is Jason Diaz. He convinces himself that he is not Eddie Leonard—that somewhere a family is waiting for him. He sets off to track down the Diaz family. He finds them relatively easily, but being accepted by them is another matter. The Diazes are now divorced and are understandably suspicious of Eddie, having waited 12 years for Jason to return. Miller Diaz, Jason's younger sister, now takes up the story. She is both attracted to and repelled by Eddie, who insists that he is Jason, who was only 3 years old when he disappeared. She thinks of Jason as her perfect brother, "even his faults were perfect" (*Leonard,* 37). In many ways, she resents this brother she had never known. She resents that he is special to her parents in a way that nobody else is. Suddenly, she must try to connect her memories of the infant Jason with this new, teenage Jason.

When Eddie first confronts Dr. Bruce Diaz, Jason's father, he is told to leave. On his way out the door, Eddie falls and is injured. Connie, Jason's mother, persuades Bruce to bring Jason to meet her. She decides to let him stay. She vacillates from being convinced that he is Jason to being sure that he is not. Lucinda Snyder, in a review in *School Library Journal,* suggests that this focus on "the search for psychological rather than physical evidence about the boy's identity" makes the story "somewhat unconvincing."[13] But it is not surprising that Connie would not really want to know the truth. After 12 years of not knowing what happened to her son, she wants to believe that Eddie is Jason. Miller begins to have doubts before Connie does:

> "I used to think when I was little that Jason was mad at us and had gone around the block to stay with a friend. Then I got older and kids teased me and said my brother was never coming back. I remember, once, someone telling me you can't hope forever. But people who say that don't know. You can hope forever. You do, don't you? You never stop waiting and hoping."
> "He's a nice boy. I like him better each day."
> "Mom, how are we going to know?"
> "We will. I'll know what I feel, what my heart says."

Oh, great! Her mother's heart was just what Eddie was always working on. (*Leonard,* 99)

By the end of the novel, Bruce Diaz has Eddie investigated, and we learn with the Diazes that he is not really Jason. After Eddie returns from a rock concert at which Miller is nearly trampled to death, he reflects on who he is:

> In the house the lights were on in every room. . . . I was hungry and drank from the juice pitcher. I felt like a burglar. *You don't belong here.* I gobbled bread down, as if someone was going to snatch it away from me. *This isn't your food, this isn't your house.* I stuffed a hunk of cheese in my pocket and went back upstairs and packed my knapsack. I left a note. "Good-bye. Thanks for everything. I still love you." (*Leonard,* 170)

But this is not the end of the novel. In the final few chapters Eddie finds a job as a painter, and one day several months later meets Miller in the mall. She calls him Jason and tells Connie that she has seen him. Connie telephones him:

> "This is hard," she said. Then abruptly, "I need to come clean with you. How can I say it to you without hurting you more? I'm just going to say it. I know you want to come back. I'm right, aren't I?" . . . "What I'm trying to say is that you're still important to me. If you ever need anything. . . . It isn't as if you're a stranger—" (*Leonard,* 183–84)

Eddie is hurt. He wants Connie to tell him to come home. He hangs up.

Eddie finally tells Phil, his boss and best friend, about Jason Diaz and his family. Only then does he begin to realize that he has made a new life for himself. He has a best friend, and his best friend's girlfriend is his friend, too. Then he thinks about all of the other friends he is making. And, someday, he thinks, maybe Miller can be his friend. When he meets a girl he likes, he thinks about telling her he is Jason Diaz. What girl would be interested in a boy named Eddie Leonard, a high school dropout with no parents and only a crazy grandmother who is dead? Finally he tells her that his name is Eddie Leonard. When she says his name aloud, he thinks, "It sounded good when she said it" (*Leonard,* 188). With these words, we finally know that Eddie has come to terms with who he is and that he can begin to rely on himself.

Mazer may take his own advice and "Kill off parents," but he recognizes that growth occurs when the events of our lives and our inner lives connect with people who care about us. For example, in *Who Is Eddie Leonard?* Phil listens sympathetically to Eddie's story and then lets him know that he's a real friend by saying: "I want to tell you one more thing. I'm your best friend, but you call me up this late again and I'm going to break your neck" (*Leonard,* 195).

4. Seeking an Identity

One of the major tasks of an adolescent is to ask, "Who am I? What is my place in the world?" The process of seeking one's identity often leads teenagers down dangerous paths, paths that can lead to addictions, crime, or premature parenthood. Most authors of books for adolescents agree that one of their important roles is to provide teenage readers with protagonists who ask these questions and make mistakes but survive to enter adulthood. Harry Mazer's protagonists are faced with questions about their own identities. They struggle to find themselves apart from families who do not share their dreams and aspirations. When they are on the threshold of achieving their dreams, they run from them. They place themselves in situations of extreme hardship in order to escape fears of failure. They attempt to become adults by trying to live in worlds that are not their own, posing to be someone other than who they are. They explore their inner worlds, dreaming of acheivement and conquest. They seek to understand their sexuality, equating maturity with sexual activity. Mazer's protagonists are normal, healthy adolescents struggling to find themselves in worlds they know well—but from which they have become alienated.

A Son's Dreams, a Father's Reality

Harry Mazer was one of two children of immigrant parents. And, like the children of many immigrants, he sought his identity in a culture that was torn between two worlds. Harry dreamed of being a writer, while his father wanted him to be financially independent and gain a trade. Sam Mazer's goals for his son were what he saw as the good life, but Harry wanted a different life. "Don't be a fool. Learn a trade," Harry remembers his father saying, "With a trade in your hands, you're a free man. A writer is a fool" (Illinois Librarians).

Harry and his father were often in conflict. Although Sam Mazer was a quiet man and Harry rarely knew what he was thinking, he let his son know in subtle ways that he was not pleased with the path the boy was taking. It was Harry's dreams—often countered by an inner voice telling him his dreams were foolish—that occupied Harry during his teenage years and even into his adulthood.

Harry Mazer's life in a family of immigrants with conflicting values and dreams is reflected in his novels. In his first novel, *Guy Lenny,* 12-year-old Guy is caught between his father, with whom he has lived since his parents' divorce, and his mother, who suddenly reenters his life. Like young Harry, Guy sees his parents as having very different values. Jean, Guy's mother, has left him with his father to go off to seek her own life. Guy can't imagine how a mother could do this. Guy and his father, Al, have found a life together that Guy thinks of in terms of shared fishing trips. Although he misses his mother, his relationship with his father has been good. Now things are beginning to change. He thinks of himself as a ball in a ping-pong game. His father has met Emily, and every time that Guy and his father plan things, Emily is included. Guy is angry with his father, and Emily accuses him of sulking.

His friends are changing, too. His childhood friend Maureen is into things Guy does not understand: smoking, going out with older boys, and sassing her mother. Mazer recalls that the scene in which Guy tells Maureen not to smoke comes directly from his own life. He remembers a girl who was the daughter of his mother's friend. Harry used to light his mother's cigarettes, and he would go out behind their apartment building and smoke. One day this girl came along and told him how stupid smoking was. He remembered that incident and put it in *Guy Lenny.* Maureen is no longer interested in hanging out with Guy; she wants to go to the pool to meet Freddy Cannon, who enjoys tormenting Guy.

Then, when it seems things couldn't get worse, Guy's mother, Jean, calls and says she is coming to town to see him. At first Guy tries to avoid her, but finally he and Jean go out to dinner. He is just beginning to feel comfortable with her when her husband, Charles, shows up. She asks Guy to come to live with them, saying that Al, Guy's father, has written to her and asked her to take Guy. Guy is hurt, confronts his father, and learns that he did write to Jean. Emily tells Guy that she and Al want to get married, but Al says that it is Guy's decision where he wants to live and that he won't try to force him to live with Jean and Charles.

When Jean comes to the apartment to have dinner, she begins to straighten Guy's things. She's critical of the lack of books and of how things haven't changed; she's critical of Emily's bowling trophy being there. Emily comes home to fix dinner and justifies what they are eating. As dinner ends, Al begins to talk to Guy about his living with his mother. He makes it clear that despite what he said before, it is not Guy's choice, "I've got to have my own life."[1]

Guy calls his father a liar and a cheat. Al slaps Guy, and Guy lashes back. After punching at his father and knocking over the pitcher of milk, he runs out of the apartment. He runs until he gets to a cemetery across from his old elementary school; there he lies in a crypt thinking about dying. He thinks of ghosts and spirits. When no one answers his call, he calls out:

> "Me. Guy Lenny.
> "Guy Lenny. GUY LENNY IS HERE. You hear me?
> "GUY LENNY IS HERE." (113)

But who is Guy Lenny? He no longer knows. Like most young people, his image of who he is has been connected to the parent with whom he has lived. Now this parent does not want him in his life: "Living with his father for seven years has created a kind of security, and faced with leaving his dad who intends to remarry and living with his mom who is remarried leads to emotional turmoil."[2]

After a long time, Guy finally returns to the apartment. His father grabs him by the arm, but his mother embraces him. Guy remembers how separate and free he'd felt the day he found an old silo. He begins to believe he is free from all of them—that he doesn't need any of them to know who he is. The adults in the book seem to believe that Guy will be just fine. As the book ends, the reader is unsure. As critic Judith Higgins suggests, Guy is "right in this book—young and tough, but not quite tough enough."[3] Guy has found answers about the conflicts within himself, between himself and his parents, and between his parents. He has not yet answered the questions: Who am I? What is my place in the world?

Perhaps it is the conflict between Mazer's dreams and his father's reality that makes fathers, or the lack of fathers, such an important part of Mazer's work. "I didn't realize when I started to write that the issue of the relationship of the father and the son would be central to so many, many of my books" (interview with author). Today he realizes that the relationship young men have with their fathers is critical in the development of their own identities. "Fathers and sons. Sons and fathers. It's a subject I'll never be free of. My father with his damped-down expectations. Don't try to be too big. Don't think you're anything special."[4]

Beginning with Mazer's first novel, *Guy Lenny,* the character of the father and the subject of the son's relationship with his father is an important theme in his books. *Guy Lenny* begins with what appears to be an idyllic relationship between a father and son, the two of them on the river together. No relationship is that perfect, and by the end of the novel Guy and his father are physically and emotionally separated.

In *The Dollar Man,* Marcus is searching for an idyllic relationship with his father. However, Marcus's father has never been part of his life; he deserted Sally, Marcus's mother, when he found out she was pregnant. When Marcus finally meets his father, his father pushes Marcus away and tries to buy his silence. Marcus learns that not all people are capable of having meaningful relationships. Leaving the money his father has given him to "buy him off" on the bus is symbolic of his understanding of this flaw in his father's character.

Running Away from Our Dreams

In *The War on Villa Street,* Willis's father pursues him as Willis tries literally to run away from a father who constantly disappoints and embarrasses him. Willis is a runner, and the symbolism of losing his first track meet when he sees his drunk father in the bleachers and later running away from home to remove himself from the stark reality of his life is not lost on teenage readers, who often look at running away as the ultimate solution. However, Willis, like most adolescents, learns that he cannot escape; he must return and face his life. When he arrives home, his mother is waiting for him. She is relieved to see him, and he learns that his father also has been worried about him. One day his father asks Willis if he hates him. Willis has grown in his understanding of his father's problems, and he answers, "I don't hate you, Pop" (181).

> Every moment of his life his father had been there in his mind, leaning on him, getting to him. It was either love or hate. He had never been free of his father. Where was his father? What was he doing? What were people saying about him? Was he drunk or sober, dead or alive?
>
> No more. No more. Please, no more. He wanted to be free of all that. He had to be free, or he couldn't live. Oddly, thinking that, he felt sorry for his father. (181–82)

It is at this moment that Willis begins to gain his freedom from his father. He leaves their apartment, and by the time he is on the street, he realizes that he is whistling. Freedom comes not from running away but from understanding the problems that cause him to want to run away.

In some of Mazer's later novels, including the second novel about Willis, *The Girl of His Dreams,* the relationships between fathers and sons are not perfect, but they are more balanced. Willis is on his own in the second novel. He is working in a factory and has come to understand some of his father's problems. When his parents come to visit him unexpectedly, Willis finds himself feeling sorry for his father. And, although he is reluctant, he agrees to have his girlfriend, Sophie, meet his parents. They take to her immediately. Later in the evening Willis and his father talk about the factory, about Willis's job, and about some of the people they know. Although his father is still critical of Willis—for example, complaining about the way he dresses, much as Mazer's father always complained about how he dressed—their relationship is that of two mature men.

But Willis still has not escaped from his father's limited dreams for him. He runs every day, and Sophie convinces him to begin training. When it appears that Willis will finally get a chance to prove his skill as a runner, he throws Sophie aside and gives up his dream; he quits training. Later, when he realizes that Sophie has left town, he begins to understand what he has done. He starts training again and convinces himself that Sophie will show up at the meet. He comes in second in the race, losing only to the great Aaron Hill. Although Sophie is not there, Willis begins to understand that his dream is possible. At the same time, he recognizes that without the encouragement of Sophie he would never have entered the race. Finally he is getting free of his father; he is still himself, but he has learned that he can become more:

> He was still Willis Pierce, but he was different.
> He'd done something that he'd never thought he could do. He'd proved something to himself. He could change. He'd run the race, he'd run against Aaron Hill. He'd done something he'd dreamed of and been afraid of. He'd done it to prove to her that he didn't have to be the way he was, that he could do something else, be somebody else.[5]

In *City Light,* the relationship between George Farina and his father is also strained, but it is not atypical. George's dreams for himself and his father's dreams for him differ. His father wants George to take over the beauty salon he owns. George would rather do almost anything else. This is not unlike an incident Mazer remembers from his youth, when a gifted friend went to a vocational high school to please his laborer father, denying his own dreams. Nor is it unlike Harry's conflict between his dream to be a writer and Sam Mazer's "damped-down expectations" for him.

When Mazer began college, he stayed only one day and then quit to enlist in the Army Air Corps. He remembers that his mother was really upset and wanted to know why he didn't wait to be drafted like all the other boys. She thought her son was wasting his brain. Mazer now realizes that—like Jack Raab in his autobiographical novel *The Last Mission*—he was not enlisting simply to fight the Nazis; he was running away from his own fears that he might not succeed in college and that his father's limited expectations for him might be correct.

After Mazer returned from Europe, he did attend and graduate from college. After college, however, he followed his father's advice and took up a trade. Much the same happens to George in *City Light*. After Julie (his girlfriend since childhood) dumps him, he begins to question the comfortable niche his father has carved out for him in a beauty salon. Almost by accident, he discovers that he enjoys refinishing furniture and working with his hands. After an argument with his father (and meeting Rosemary, a dancer, through a bulletin board on his sister's computer network) he moves out of his home and goes to work refinishing furniture:

> A year ago, six months ago, I didn't know her. I'd had my life all figured out. All the pieces in place. George going in a totally different direction. It was George and Julie forever. We were going to college together. Eventually I'd go to work for my father, someday own the business. At some point, Julie would open a medical office and we'd get married and settle down here or in Englewood, or if we could afford it, North Park. And now everything had changed.
>
> Julie and I were going our own ways. I was working, getting involved with wood and old furniture. Was that going to be my life? And Rosemary—she was in my life somehow, but I wasn't completely sure how. I didn't see us fitting neatly together. She

was an artist. I was—at this point—a furniture stripper. Would I do it all my life? And where was my life going to be? Clifton Heights? New York City? Los Angeles? Someplace I hadn't even thought of yet?[6]

By the end of the novel, George and his father begin to come to terms with each other. Mr. Farina toasts George at his eighteenth birthday dinner: "To my son, George, who is in charge of his life now" (200). Things are still cool between father and son as they leave the restaurant. As they walk down the street, George turns to his father and says,

"I love you, Dad."
"Well," he said. "Well, You've got some way of showing it."
But he put his arm around my shoulders and kept it there all the way back to the car. (202)

Religion and the Teenager

One of the major tasks for adolescents when seeking their identity is to explore a personal commitment to religion or a spiritual self. The conflicts between young Harry Mazer's dreams, his mother's dream for him, and his father's reality were compounded by his family's old world ways and their Jewishness. Growing up as the child of Polish immigrant Jews was not easy even in a neighborhood where other children came from similar backgrounds. Although Mazer claims to remember little anti-Semitism, he does recall being very aware that he was Jewish and understanding that to be Jewish was to be different—less American, in his opinion. In most ways, his parents' and other relatives' lives were similar to those their parents and grandparents had lived as Jews in Polish villages. They were factory workers, shopkeepers, peddlers, chicken farmers, and secretaries.

Mazer left his Jewish world by hiding his Judaism when he entered Union College. This was his rebellion against his past. Strangely, he has never dealt with this aspect of his identity in his novels. His characters are Jewish, but their Jewishness has almost no impact on the stories—except for Jack, who wants to fight Hitler to avenge what the Nazis are doing to the Jews of Europe. But even Jack's Jewishness is not explored. Mazer says that this is one aspect of his own life that he has not yet fully examined; only in the past several years, since he and Norma have moved back to New York City for a part of each year, has he begun to think of himself as a Jew. Perhaps a future book will have a protagonist who must come to terms with being Jewish in American society.

Socioeconomic Status and the Teenager's Identity

Although Mazer's Jewishness is not explored in his novels, his economic and social backgrounds are. The socioeconomic environment in which his teenage protagonists live is important to their identities. In fact, critics have referred to Mazer's novels as working-class literature. The adult characters in his novels work as unskilled laborers. His adolescent protagonists dream of a better life but, like Mazer, have parents who reject their aspirations. Often his leads characters to run away because they are afraid that their parents might be right, they might fail. Mazer's protagonists usually have no adults who model how to reach their goals. Marcus knows no one who is a writer, and Willis knows no other runners. They appear condemned to lives similar to those of their parents.

Willis is 18 at the beginning of *The Girl of His Dreams*. He poses as a famous runner, running miles each day, but he has no idea how to achieve his dream; the word *college* is not even in the vocabulary of this young factory worker who has rejected but then settles for a life like his father's.

Jeff in *Hey, Kid! Does She Love Me?* has just graduated from high school. His parents and siblings think he should go to college, but his dream is to earn enough money by working as a dishwasher and as a house painter so that he can travel to California to pursue a life in the movies. Jeff spends much of his time thinking in movie scenes; he poses in all types of scenarios. Much of the book is told in Jeff's voice from the perspective of Jeff as great movie producer and leading man. Although Jeff helps Mary, the love of his life, regain her dream of an acting career after an unwanted pregnancy and the birth of her baby, Hannah, he seems to be stuck in a rut, working at menial jobs. Finally, Jeff decides that he must go to California if he is ever to realize his dream. He says good-bye to his parents and leaves on a bus heading west. The book ends with two letters: one from Mary telling Jeff how much he means to her—how without him she wouldn't be where she is now—and the other from Jeff telling Mary that he is working his way up from the bottom, that he spent several days sleeping on the beach with other would-be directors and actors "waiting to be famous."[7] After money from his sister Natalie helps him, he tells Mary he is working his way up in the movies, beginning as a dishwasher in the studio cafeteria, now working on the food line and applying for a security job; he is also taking acting lessons at night. Like Mazer, Jeff learns that the only way to realize a dream is to pursue it and to gain the skills needed to achieve it.

Tolley and Bubber in *Cave under the City* are brothers who live in a housing project known as the "co-ops"—almost mirroring Harry Mazer's young life. However, unlike Harry, Tolley and Bubber are left parentless when their father goes to Baltimore in an attempt to find a job as a house painter and their mother is hospitalized with tuberculosis. Tolley and Bubber seek their own identities while trying to hide from social services and survive with little money and only minimal shelter on the streets and in the cellars of New York City during the Depression.

Even the protagonists who grow up among the privileged wealthy and whose parents share their dreams are on their own to achieve them. Cleo in *The Island Keeper* is sent to private boarding schools and summer camps after her mother is killed in a freak accident. She sees her father and grandmother as insensitive and uncaring—not models for the person she is struggling to become. Derek in Norma and Harry Mazer's *Solid Gold Kid* is loved by his divorced parents but spends most of his time in boarding schools. His father is one of the wealthiest men in the country, but Derek tries to hide from the wealth so that he can be accepted for who he is. It is his father's great wealth that nearly costs him and several adolescents he has just met their lives. Like the brothers in *Cave under the City,* in *When the Phone Rang* the three Keller siblings try to survive on their own after their parents are killed in a plane crash while returning from a vacation in Bermuda. The Keller children are not poor, but like most of Mazer's protagonists, they are left without role models.

Becoming a Man

For many adolescent boys, the way to become a man is to assume the roles of a man, at times before one is prepared. Mazer entered the army at 17 not only to escape from his father and his own fears about whether or not he could achieve his dreams but also to learn what it is to be a man. When he enlisted in the Army Air Corps, he took on a new set of dreams: He wanted to become a pilot and a conquering hero. Instead, he found the harsh realities of death and war. Like his fictional hero Jack Raab in *The Last Mission,* Mazer sought his identity, attempting to discover what it means to be a man, in the world of the wartime armed forces. Unlike Jack, who is only 15 and lies in order to enlist, he did not enter the war without his family's knowledge; but Mazer, too, was running away. Neither Mazer nor Jack became a conquering hero. Instead, they watched their buddies die in the last mission they flew over Czechoslovakia. To this day, Mazer is attempting to deal with this loss.

Mazer says he wrote *The Last Mission* to help him answer questions that have continued to haunt him. Why had he survived? Why had the others died? Did they have to fly that last mission? Was there any meaning to what they had done? Any meaning to those deaths, to all the other deaths of World War II? Today, he is still searching for answers to these questions—and still writing about his personal war.

In many ways, Jack Raab in *The Last Mission* learns what it is to become a man. He learns about friendship and loss. He learns about survival under extremely difficult conditions. He understands that war is not about becoming a hero but is about death and destruction. He learns about fear and bravery and recognizes that both can exist in the same man. However, like Mazer, Raab has not answered the question of why he survived when the others died. Nor has he learned whether their deaths were worthwhile. These are the lessons of a lifetime. Jack knows at the end of the novel that his search for the answers to these questions will be ongoing.

The Inner Life and the Search for Identity

Mazer's adolescent dreams and posing allowed him to escape from what he saw as the limited aspirations of his father. Today, it is this inner life that connects him with the young adults who read his novels. He celebrates the inner lives of his characters and advises teachers of adolescents to do the same. According to Mazer, it is the inner lives of adolescents that allow them to become whatever they dream: "Posing, assuming a persona, creating a character could be the beginning of authorship, which is nothing if it's not making up characters and playing parts."[8]

The characters in each of Mazer's novels have their own inner lives. Marcus in *I Love You, Stupid!* has an inner life in which he is a writer and a great lover. In an earlier novel about Marcus, *The Dollar Man,* 13-year-old Marcus has an inner life with a father he has never known, a father who is good, kind, rich, brave, and famous. His father, he later learns, is none of these.

Willis in *The War on Villa Street* dreams of being a great runner despite his meager existence and his alcoholic father. An older Willis in *The Girl of His Dreams* has not yet forsaken his dream of running, even though he is an 18-year-old who spends his days working in a factory. In fact, his dream of running encourages him to pose as a runner at a college track meet, and it is this posing and the realistic love of Sophie Brown that changes his life.

George in *City Lights* dreams of his life with Julie. Jeff Orloff in *Hey, Kid! Does She Love Me?* dreams of being loved by Mary

Silver and having a career as a filmmaker. His dreams take the form of movie scripts that he plays out in his head. *In Who Is Eddie Leonard?* Eddie dreams of being Jason Diaz, the boy on the missing-child poster. Both Sam and Lisa in *Someone's Mother Is Missing* dream of being in families that are different from their own. Cleo Murphy in *The Island Keeper* not only dreams of being independent of her father and grandmother but also becomes so by running away to a deserted island. Jack Raab does the same in *The Last Mission*. (The inner worlds of Mazer's characters are discussed in more depth in Chapter 2.)

Mazer's teenage dreams were in many ways more real to him than the real world in which he lived. He enacted his dreams by posing. He became a writer by posing as one, not by being one. As an adult author, Mazer gives this same sense of frustration—of a dream impossible to realize—to his character Marcus in *I Love You, Stupid!*

Mazer says that, like many teenagers, he had no idea that writing required talent; neither does Marcus, who wants to drop out of school so that he can write. Marcus tells his friend Wendy that he is going to be a writer: "'I'm going to write,' he said to Wendy. His whole life would be reorganized around writing. No more screwing around panting after girls, wasting his life. He had purpose. School was irrelevant, the courses he was taking—trig, chemistry, even the diploma—all irrelevant. 'If you know where you're going you go there. Everything else is irrelevant'" (52).

Like Mazer as a young man, Marcus assumed that writing was largely inspiration. Both of them had to learn that writing, though partly a matter of talent, is largely a matter of hard work. One cannot write without living life and learning—always learning. The more you live, the more you know and the better you write. "Everything in my life prepared me for being a writer," says Mazer. "All my books grow out of my life and my family and people I meet. But also from my dreams, imaginings, worries and broodings and things I can't get out of my head."[9]

Although Marcus dreamed of being and a writer, he, like Mazer (see Chapter 7), was taught what it takes to become a writer by a woman. Sally, Marcus's mother, made it clear that dropping out

of school was not the best path to becoming a writer. But Sally,
like all good mentors, understands that you can't thwart a young
man's dream. Instead, she suggests a compromise. Marcus can
drop the courses he does not need for graduation, rearrange his
schedule, and come home in the afternoons to write. Marcus is
not surprised by Sally's compromise—he thinks of her as the
great compromiser—but even as he underestimates the importance of her help, he grows in his respect for her. It is Sally who
begins to teach Marcus that a dream cannot be realized without
work, without effort, and without talent.

Love, Sex, and the Teenager

Mazer as a teenager also sought his identity by dreaming of relationships with the beautiful Isabels in his classes. His dreams of
sex and love were an important part of his inner life, but only his
inner life—not his real life. The Isabel whom Mazer writes about
appears twice in his novels. She appears first as Vivian in *The
Dollar Man,* when 13-year-old Marcus Rosenbloom stands on a
cold city sidewalk looking longingly into the windows of her
apartment. She appears again in *The War on Villa Street* as one of
the girls who taunt young Willis.

In *I Love You, Stupid!* 17-year-old Marcus remembers another
Isabel, another dream unfulfilled, this time in the person of Isabel
Malefsky, a girl in his sixth-grade class who has become the
antagonist of a story he is writing about unrequited love, symbolized by a rejected Valentine's Day card. Mazer says that this is a
different girl and that the story is a fantasy; but like all the girls
in his books, she is someone from his life. He remembers the pain
not merely of being rejected by girls but also of not knowing even
how to approach them. He recalls: "I was very awkward with
girls. I didn't talk to girls. I didn't have anything to do with girls"
(interview with author).

There is no doubt that for many adolescents the inner world is
far more appealing than the real world of clumsy attempts at love
and sexual relationships. Willis and Marcus dream not only of

writing and running but also of unconquerable loves. Marcus's dreams are of sex. He dreams of both Wendy, a girl his age with whom he has a developing relationship, and Karen, an older woman for whom he baby-sits: "Marcus was in love. Or was it lust? He couldn't make up his mind. Where did love end and lust begin? 'Karen' . . . he said her name. She was perfect, she was different—those shell-like ears, that long regal nose. All his fantasies focused on Karen, in need, fragile, sensitive, helpless, turning to him" (78–79). When Marcus attempts to turn his inner desire for Karen into reality, not only does he botch his attempt; he is also rebuffed: "His hands fell to her arms. He pulled her toward him, leaned toward her, tried to kiss her" (105). She tells him to get out and never come back again—he is fired. For the adolescent, fantasy is often better than reality.

Willis's dreams are of a relationship with a beautiful girl. He's not attracted to the plain Sophie Brown, who is interested in him. After a rather disastrous date with Dore, the friend of the beautiful and desirable Lee, he thinks about Sophie: "Too much smile. She was all right, but she was too eager. She stood too close. She needed someone to take her aside, tell her the facts of city life" (*Girl,* 61). However, by the end of the novels, Marcus and Willis each learn that the reality of a meaningful relationship with someone who cares is more important and far better than dreams of, as Marcus says, "the three B's: bones, boobs, and butts" (*Stupid,* 44).

Perhaps because Mazer has spent much of his life attempting to discover who he is, these questions of identity are central to each of his books. All of his characters are attempting to discover who they are and where they fit into the world. In the process, they frequently stumble and fall, make poor choices, associate with the wrong people, and get themselves into many difficult and dangerous situations. But in each of Mazer's novels, the protagonist grows. By the end of the novel, the protagonist has a far better sense of her or his own identity. As Carolyn W. Carmichael suggests, all of Mazer's characters are "healthily stubborn young people, resourceful young people, and when the time comes, capable of strong if sometimes imprudent action."[10]

5. Tales of Survival and Suspense

In addition to being an author of coming-of-age novels for young adults, Harry Mazer also writes numerous suspense and survival tales. The initiation of a young person—a rite of passage—frequently requires isolation from society; a natural parallel to these books, then, is the novel of survival, in which the protagonist must overcome odds to survive in an alien environment.

According to Mazer, "On one level all my stories beginning with *Guy Lenny* and *Snow Bound* are survival stories. I am a survivor, have the survivor's mentality."[1] Mazer suggests that "life itself is a survival story. . . . The more I see, the more I live, the more I believe it's true. I came out of a family of survivors. People who, and as history has turned out, are indeed survivors. I'll never forget the number of years that distanced my parents from the holocaust in Poland. I'm talking twenty years" (interview with author). Carolyn W. Carmichael finds a "thematic similarity of survival" that ties together all of Mazer's novels.[2] Survival novels like Mazer's often have elements of suspense related to the young person's struggle to survive.

Mazer as a young man was an avid reader. However, he did not read for style or literary art. "It wasn't literature I craved but action, conflict, suspense."[3] So is it any wonder that Mazer's books for adolescents are the kind of books that would have appealed to him growing up as a reader, isolated from his family and in many ways from his peers? Five of Mazer's novels can be classified as survival novels with elements of suspense: *Snow Bound, When the Phone Rang, Someone's Mother Is Missing, The*

Island Keeper, and *The Last Mission.* However, only one, *The Solid Gold Kid,* written with his wife Norma Fox Mazer, can be classified as a suspense story.

The Suspense Story

Suspense novels for young adults have gained popularity in recent years, largely because they catch teenagers unawares and deal with the unknown. They, according to the critic Carolyn W. Carmichael, "take readers out of their ordinary lives. Lives are shifted, the familiar becomes unfamiliar, the characters find themselves in strange surroundings, challenged, tested, forced to struggle, forced to be resilient, inventive, forced to cope. AND THEY DO!"[4] Readers must suspend disbelief in order to be caught up in the spine-tingling effect of the plot. The protagonist is typically the victim or the intended victim. She or he is usually vulnerable and isolated. Readers empathize because they recognize themselves in the character's plight. The voice teenagers hear in the story is the victim's voice, and in it they hear their own voices. Although the protagonist is introduced early in the novel, it may not be until much later that his or her vulnerability is recognized.

The antagonist is usually evil and intelligent—the "crime" has yet to be committed. This person is often bold, insensitive, exceptionally cunning, insightful, manipulative, and believable, and she or he may even be a peer of the protagonist, who may or may not suspect this villain. At times, the victim will not know who the antagonist is, but the reader will. Typically, in the suspense story, we await the enactment of the evil act rather than attempting to determine who committed the crime.

The suspense story usually has a complex plot and may contain several subplots, which help to build tension and uncertainty. Character development of both the protagonist and the antagonist is central to the plot, and the author frequently provides clues that are misleading. Chapters usually begin with hooks and end with cliff-hangers to keep the reader turning the pages. The setting is important and adds to the foreboding sense of drama within the plot. Literary techniques such as foreshadowing and flashback are often employed.

The major differences between adult suspense stories and young adult suspense stories center on the age of the protagonist and the complexity of the plot. However, the reader's empathy with the protagonist, the building of suspense through various plotting techniques, and the theme that things are not always what they seem are important in both young adult and adult suspense novels.

The Solid Gold Kid

In suspense stories the protagonist is isolated, lonely, and vulnerable. In *The Solid Gold Kid* there is no doubt that Derek Chapman is isolated. Derek is a student in a private boys' school; his father is a multimillionaire—a business tycoon—who is usually too busy for his son. Derek's parents are divorced, and his mother and sister live across the country, in California. He is also isolated among the boys at his school. He's different. His father is far richer than the other students' parents, most of whom are doctors or business executives. Derek has been transferred from one prep school to another. He's more interested in bluegrass music than in membership in the exclusive Payne Club, and he has barely avoided a fistfight with Will Harmon, chairman of the Room Committee: "Hold it there, Chapman! Hold it right there. I've just come from a meeting of the Payne Club executive board. You've turned down the best club in the school. Why? Can you tell me why? Never mind, I'll tell you why. Pure, unadulterated snobbery!"[5] But it's not snobbery that has kept Derek from joining the club. Derek believes that the only reason he has been invited to join the club is his father's money:

> Nothing was going to convince Will Harmon that I'd turned down Payne Club just because I didn't want to be a snob and a phony. I'd never shown any interest in Payne Club, so why had they asked me to join? It could only be the charm of the

Chapman millions. Not one of those guys was, ever had been, or ever meant to be my friend. (*Solid,* 6)

On Saturdays, rather than hanging around campus or going home as half the other boys do, Derek takes the 12:22 bus to Simon's to listen to bluegrass music. He's interested in girls but has not had much success with them.

Derek's isolation is more keenly felt because the authors tell his story in the first person. He is alone with his own thoughts even after he becomes caught up with five kids he had never before met on a particularly eventful Saturday afternoon.

On this rainy Saturday on the way to the bus, Derek sees a pretty blond girl leaving Payne Lecture Hall. The girl, a townie who had been attending a Saturday lecture along with a lot of other kids, is on her way to the bus stop. When Derek and the five others who are waiting for the bus accept a ride in a gray van, we want to say to them, "How dumb can you be?" However, we know that Derek's asking for the lift downtown is a way to make him appear heroic to the girl, who does not want to wait for the bus in the rain. The Mazers have set the scene for the beginning of a terrifying tale of suspense: a lonely exceptionally wealthy young man, a beautiful girl, a nearly deserted campus, a rainy Saturday, and a gray paneled van.

The major weakness of this suspense novel is the antagonists. Although they are certainly cruel and terrifying, they are less convincing because they are neither as cunning nor as intelligent as the antagonists in such books as Lois Duncan's *Killing Mr. Griffin* or Robert Cormier's *After the First Death.* They need to be developed more fully in order to be scarier. We know immediately that the crime is not well planned when they allow all five adolescents to enter their van rather than waiting for a time when they find Derek alone. They are far too anxious, and not nearly cunning enough to be truly frightening.

As the reviewer Jack Forman says in a *School Library Journal* review, the kidnappers are "drawn broadly."[6] We never get to know them, nor do we ever see them as real people, thereby limiting our terror. They are the stereotypical, television version of evil, and they are almost comic in their stupidity:

> They dropped me. Birds were singing. The fields smelled of manure. I looked up at them. She was wearing the belted trench coat, the red scarf. He had on a fringed jacket. His face was puffy. They didn't look evil, only ordinary.
>
> My heart jerked behind my ribs. He bent over, pushing me, rolling me deeper into the underbrush like a bundle of rags. I saw his face over me. Those narrow squeezed-up eyes. Sweat poured off his face. He raised his gun. (*Solid,* 163)

From an earlier conversation between Bogie and Pearl (the kidnappers), we know that they do not know what to do with Derek; nor are they afraid to let him know who they are.

Bogie is certainly evil. He seems to care only about what he can earn from the "caper," and that's how he views the kidnapping. However, he is also bumbling and stupid. In the end, he is unable to kill Derek because he has forgotten to load his gun. It is clear that Pearl is the brain behind the kidnapping, but she does not have the persuasive power to prevent Bogie from making errors of brute force, nor is she able to see beyond getting the ransom money. Their stupidity and poor planning allow Derek to escape, but these characteristics also keep the reader from fearing them.

In the most suspenseful of suspense novels, the protagonist knows the antagonist quite well but has no idea of the evil that lies within. The reader, however, begins to recognize the danger through clues introduced by the author that are not evident to the vulnerable victim. This is certainly true of the relationship in Duncan's *Killing Mr. Griffin* between Mark, the psychotic whom the adolescent Susan almost begins to love; and Susan, the vulnerable, unattractive girl. However, in *The Solid Gold Kid* the reader knows almost immediately that the driver and the passenger in the van in which the students accept a ride have evil intentions, and it doesn't take long for the adolescent characters to figure this out as well:

"I said I'd give you a ride, Derek, not the whole freaking school."
"Oh, if that's the way it is," the blond girl said, "I'll walk."
She started to get down.
"Me too," I said quickly, starting to follow her.
"No you don't," the woman said. She thrust the girl back into the van and slammed the door. (13)

The story would have been much more terrifying if the antagonists had been known to Derek before the kidnapping and had not made their intentions so obvious so early.

The plot of *The Solid Gold Kid* works largely because of the supporting cast of characters. "The kids (all conveniently representing different backgrounds) are developed with empathy and understanding."[7] Each, as Jack Forman points out, "loses control at least once, and each has a turn at heroics." The plot occurs over six days, during which the adolescents go from relatively carefree, normal kids to terrified victims who must fight for their survival. During the ordeal, they come to hate, love, and finally appreciate one another. They are beaten, starved, tied, gagged, threatened, and moved from place to place in the back of a dark, dirty van. Throughout the ordeal, they experience peer pressure typical of adolescents, and a relationship begins to form between Derek and Pam. Jeff is blinded in a fire that they set in an attempt to escape from a stone bathhouse; Wendy's beloved dog is brutally killed as an example of what might happen to them; Pam is shot trying to escape and is left for dead; and Ed is eventually locked in the van and left to starve. Another almost successful escape attempt from a fire tower is foiled when Derek and Ed are run down and caught by Bogie and Pearl. Jeff, who is blind, and Wendy run into the woods and pelt the van with rocks, causing Bogie to fire shots randomly at them through the trees. Ed and Derek do not know whether they are dead or alive. The plot is fast-paced. Although many of the sophisticated elements of suspense—such as flashbacks and foreshadowing—are missing, the story is frightening enough to keep readers turning pages.

Survival Stories

Survival books are a popular subgenre of the suspense novel. The difference between suspense stories and survival stories is not in the suspense they create but in *what* creates it. In survival stories, the suspense is created as the characters are forced to overcome the difficulties of their natural environments and day-to-day lives. There is no villain. Often the evil that must be overcome is not caused by human beings and frequently lurks within the weakness or fear of the protagonist. Many teenagers like to imagine what it would be like if they were caught in a situation in which they must use ingenuity and strength to free themselves. It is no wonder that such stories are very popular with adolescents, because they show how ordinary young adults overcome extraordinary situations.

Isolation of the protagonist is one of the most important elements of survival tales. Harry Mazer's protagonists are all isolated. He wonders aloud why this is so: "Maybe because I'm Jewish . . . grew up during the Depression . . . the Second World War . . . maybe because I was shot down during World War II. . . . Survivors take nothing for granted, expect the worst, persist. . . . It's an uncertain world. We all live in the shadow of a holocaust so vast it's beyond our powers to comprehend. There is no end to the uncertainty, especially for the young."[8]

In *Snow Bound,* Tony and Cindy are caught on a country road in a raging blizzard. Cindy is injured in the wreck that has stranded their car on the desolate Tug Hill plateau of upper New York State. She can't walk, and Tony goes off through the white world to seek help. Soon both of the characters are completely alone, facing death but trying to survive in a cold, alien world.

One of the reasons both Tony and Cindy work as characters in a survival story is that they are both real people with real strengths and weaknesses. Norma recalls that this almost didn't happen. Norma and Harry have always been the first readers of each other's novels. When Norma first read *Snow Bound,* she was not happy with the character of Cindy. "She just started crying," Norma says. Harry admits that Cindy in the initial draft was "just a big cliché." Harry says that he has a tendency to do what is easiest and that creating something fresh—something that hasn't been seen or heard before—is hard, tiring work. In order to make Cindy more than a cliché, he had to think, and think hard. He had to make her more than a girl who simply cries when confronted by a difficult problem; she had to become a protagonist who could stand up to her problems and defeat them. That is why *Snow Bound* is such a good survival story. We know that Cindy is the kind of person who can survive her own isolation, and she is the kind of person whom we want to see survive.

Cleo's mother and beloved sister, Jam, in *The Island Keeper* have both been killed in freak accidents: her mother while running away with her daughters from an unhappy marriage, and Jam in an unexplained boating accident at camp. Now Cleo lives with her grandmother and her rich father. To Cleo's mind, she is not what they wanted her to be. They are rich, very rich; but her father, who has a lot of principles, tells her never to "flaunt your wealth. Don't show off. Don't act better than anyone else." Her grandmother wants her to be feminine, but Cleo prefers jeans and plaid shirts. Her grandmother wants her to be pretty and a lady, but Cleo is overweight and doesn't eat the way her grandmother thinks she should. She feels unloved by her grandmother and distant from her father. Cleo turns to food when she is nervous or scared, which is often. She has to get away, and so she plans "eight steps to freedom." The first step is not going to the camp her grandmother has arranged for her to attend this summer— calling the camp director and in her grandmother's voice telling the director that "Cleo wasn't returning to camp this summer" (21). Harry has set the scene for the survival tale: a lonely, isolated, unattractive girl running away from home.

Eddie Leonard in *Who Is Eddie Leonard?* is also isolated. He lives with his grandmother and footloose uncle, but he never feels as though he is part of his abusive family. He doesn't believe the story his grandmother tells him about Sharon, the mother who deserted him, because he has caught his grandmother in so many lies. After his grandmother dies, Eddie lives alone for a while in the walk-up apartment and tries to contact his Uncle Stew. Eddie is desperately lonely. When his grandmother's cat, Siam, is lost, Eddie goes to the post office to put up a sign, and he comes upon a poster about a missing child—Jason Diaz. He tears the poster down and takes it home. One day he holds the poster to his face as he looks in the mirror: *"I belong to that face. I belong to a family. I belong somewhere else. Not here. Not to my grandmother who's gone, not to Sharon who never was, not to Uncle Stew, who never came"* (*Leonard*, 33). Eddie decides to end his isolation by leaving the apartment and searching for the Diaz family.

Tolley Holtz and his 5-year-old brother, Bubber, in *Cave under the City* are also alone. It is during the Great Depression; their father is searching for work in another city, and their mother is hospitalized. Tolley takes Bubber to Grandmother Buba's, hoping that she will care for them; but she, too, is ill. Tolley tries to see his mother to find out where his father is, but the hospital will not let the boys go to her room. When they are turned over to social services, by the concerned hospital staff, Tolley quickly figures out that they will be placed in foster care, and so he and Bubber flee. Now they are without parents, have no family, and have almost no money. How will they survive?

The Keller children in *When the Phone Rang* are also parentless. One minute their parents are on their way home from a vacation in Bermuda; the next minute, Billy Keller learns that they have been killed in a plane crash. Billy's younger sister, Lori, won't believe her parents are dead, and his older brother, Kevin, is forced to return home from college, which he does begrudgingly. Grandma Betty, Uncle Paul, and Aunt Joan arrive to care for the family. From the beginning, things are strained. Uncle Paul does not approve of the slow progress the Kellers have made on remodeling their home; Aunt Joan wants the children to dress for dinner. They criticize what and how the children eat:

> "If you're leaving the table, Lori," Aunt Joan said, "you should excuse yourself. Your mother, I know, taught you manners."
>
> "Yes, she did." Lori's eyes were shut tight. "She taught us thoughtfulness and consideration for other people's feelings."[9]

The day after the memorial service—as Aunt Joan is packing glasses and the children learn for the first time of Paul's and Joan's intention to move them—Billy begins to think, "If Kevin stays, we can stay" (39). Billy tells Kevin and is himself told to slow down—everything is already worked out. Billy will go with Aunt Joan and Uncle Paul, who have sons, and Lori will go with Grandma Betty; Kevin will go back to college. Billy makes it clear that they do not want to go: "You've got it wrong, Uncle Paul," I said. "You don't have to come back. You don't have to worry about us. If Kevin stays home, we can stay together in this house" (44). Kevin says he can't do that. Billy runs out of the house, saying, "You pig. You're letting them split us up. Lori in one place. Me another. We're not even a family anymore" (45). Kevin and Billy go for a ride. Billy convinces Kevin to stay; they come back and convince Joan and Paul to let them stay alone. Suddenly, the three Keller children are faced with surviving on their own together.

Lisa and her younger sister Robyn are also left parentless when their father dies in *Someone's Mother Is Missing*. Their cousin Sam, who shares the narration of the novel with Lisa, has always believed that his uncle is very rich. When he dies, Lisa's mother becomes more and more distant and difficult to get along with. Lisa does not realize that her mother is slowly learning that their fortune is leveraged and that they have nothing. Her mother increasingly removes herself from reality, some days not even getting out of bed. One day Sam rides his bike to Lisa's house. When he looks in, he discovers it is empty:

> Then he saw his aunt, and jumped back. She was sitting on the floor in the empty living room, her back against the wall. She wore jeans and a sweatshirt and her knees were up. She was staring straight out at him. He raised his hand in greeting. Her eyes were open, but she didn't see him. She was staring straight through him.[10]

Not long after that day, Lisa's mother disappears. At first the girls try to stay in the house alone; but as it becomes clearer that their mother is not coming back, they go to live with Sam and his family.

The Setting is Crucial

In almost all suspense novels, the setting is critical. This is okay with Mazer. He's always enjoyed developing settings. As a young college student, much of what he wrote were pieces with descriptive settings. Next to voice, he considers place the most important element of his novels.

In a suspense story, the setting does far more than show where the story takes place. It helps set the tone of the novel. Cleo's cave on Duck Island in a lake in Canada in *The Island Keeper* could not be more lonely. Although Cleo has sought her aloneness and we revel with her in her ability to conquer her problems and fears, we know the winter will come. The isolated ruggedness of this island and the danger the reader recognizes in the pending winter helps set the novel's tone of suspense.

The tone is set in the Mazers' *Solid Gold Kid* by the gray van and the even grayer day. In *Who Is Eddie Leonard?* the starkness of the conditions of the apartment in which Eddie lives helps set the tone. We know that the ringing telephone which opens *When the Phone Rang* will not bring good news for the Keller family. And *Someone's Mother Is Missing* opens with Sam and his family about to attend his uncle's funeral.

The Mazer novel that most effectively uses setting to communicate suspense is *Snow Bound*. In an argument with Ron Buehl (then editor-in-chief of Delacorte Books for Young Readers) over the title of that novel, Mazer emphasized the importance of the isolated environment. Four of the five titles Norma and Harry Mazer suggested reflect isolation: "In a Hidden Land," "Off the Road," "Two against the Cold," and "An Island in the Snow."[11] However, Buehl won the day by arguing that "Snow Bound," along with a nugget on the jacket—"a story of raw survival"— tells the reader "what the book is about without having to rely on the flap copy (which a lot of kids never bother with if the title doesn't mean anything to them)."[12] Mazer, in the letter to Buehl in which he suggested titles, also requested that a quotation appear on the title page to help set the scene:

> Without a doubt the most forbidding and unknown physiographic region in New York State is the great windswept plateau called Tug Hill. On a road map it is that strange blank area of roughly two hundred thousand acres approximately 20 miles southeast of Watertown and 30 miles northwest of Utica. An effort to locate a hamlet or even a dirt road in this enigmatic area can only be rewarded with frustration.[13]

The quotation did appear on the title page as Mazer suggested.

The settings of *The Last Mission* help provide that novel's suspense. Mazer knew all of these places well; they are places from his own experience in World War II. The book begins with Jack Raab in crew training as a tail gunner on a bomber at Alexandria Army Field in Louisiana. This is the base at which Harry met Mike Brennan, his best buddy, who became Chuckie O'Brien in the novel. In the early chapters of the novel there are flashbacks to Jack in basic training and on a date in Miami at the beach. There was a real date on Miami Beach, and the girl in the date in the book was a real girl in Mazer's life, but the events in the novel and the relationship between Jack and Dotty are fictional.

Jack and his mates have a weekend pass in the French Quarter of New Orleans. Jack, who is only 15 and has enlisted by lying about his age, spends his time in a dark movie house and calls Dotty, a New York girl he met on Miami Beach. He promises her he will see her when he is home on furlough before getting shipped abroad. Jack and his crewmate Chuckie head to New York City. Jack has grown up in a Jewish working-class neighborhood in the Bronx. Mazer knows the neighborhood of Jack's childhood well, since it is where he grew up and went to school. But Jack can't go home, although he aches to do so. He can't even call his mother. He has run away from home to enlist, and he is afraid that if his parents find him, they will report his lie. So, when Jack arrives in New York City, he decides to go to Brooklyn, where Dotty lives. We see the city through the eyes of Jack and through the eyes of Mazer. We take the Coney Island Express with him and eat hamburgers at a White Tower. We walk along the streets and see people who remind him of his parents. We feel his pain as he stays in a rooming house and attempts to get the nerve to call Dotty. We're with Jack when he drinks too much beer and gets drunk for the first time. We feel the cold damp sand under the boardwalk, where he passes out. When he finally does call Dotty, his furlough is almost over—the seventh and last day. She is upset that he didn't call earlier but agrees to spend the day with him; this is the longest time Jack has ever spent with a girl. Before he leaves, he wants to give Dotty something—a present. He takes the Star of David from around his neck, saying, "Dotty—this is for you" (57). This did not occur in Mazer's world. He never wore a Star of David. In fact, he says that he gave up his Jewish world when he entered the army; he didn't tell anyone that he was Jewish. Mazer remembers his indecision about whether to put an *H* for Hebrew on his dog tag, not because he was afraid of what might happen if he were captured but because he was not religious.

The setting of *The Last Mission* changes. No longer is the crew housed in the relative comfort of an American army base; now the men are in the freezing cold huts of the Eighth Air Force, 398th Bomb Group in England. We feel as if we are there with Jack, hating the cold and the food, feeling the fear of knowing that today will bring another flying mission. Nothing has prepared Jack or prepared us for the starkness of the place. Nothing has prepared these young men for the horror of what they are about to do:

> Jack swung out of bed. Bare feet on icy concrete floor. Concrete floors, metal walls, no heat—whoever dreamed up these Nissen huts was a fiend. He dressed quickly. All his clothes were clammy. . . .
>
> They made their way through the blackness. Not a star overhead. The chow hall was blacked out on the outside. Inside it was warm and smelled of coffee and frying eggs. The flying crews were the only ones who got real eggs. Everyone else got powdered eggs. . . .

> When the briefing officer pulled the curtain aside, Jack
> focused on the long red thread that ran across the map of
> Europe. That was their mission. A shiver went through Jack.
> "Berlin." (62–64)

We are with Jack and the crew as they prepare for their mission
and take off—one bomber every 10 seconds. We feel the cramps in
our legs as Jack crouches and the weight of the flak on our backs.
We squint through the holes in the cloud cover to see the towns
and countryside below. We fight to breathe, and we chip the ice
from our chins under the rubber masks we wear. Most of all we
feel the cold. Then, directly ahead, is Berlin. Our hearts beat fran-
tically along with Jack's. We, too, crouch down and bend over to
protect ourselves. We are terrified, but we force ourselves to keep
watching, even though we realize that the shadow which feels too
close to our position and made us duck from fear was the body of
a man falling through the air. We, like Jack, try to keep from
thinking about the burning city below. Finally, it is over, and we
breathe again, singing over the noise of the engines as we return:
"Off we go, into the wild blue yonder! Flying high . . . into the
sun!" (71).

It is clear from the vividness of his descriptions and from the
feelings they invoke in us that Mazer has been there, that he has
felt the cold and the fear. And because he has been there, he takes
us there with him and with Jack.

Overcoming the Environment

An essential element in many tales of survival is conquering a
hostile environment into which one has fallen by accident or
error. This is most evident in four of Harry Mazer's novels: *The
Island Keeper, Snow Bound, The Last Mission,* and *Cave under
the City.* In *The Island Keeper,* Cleo runs away from home and is
eventually forced to survive the approaching winter on an island
in a lake in Canada. In *Snow Bound,* Tony and Cindy must find
their way out of a New York State wilderness in a raging snow
storm. Jack Raab, in *The Last Mission,* must survive the cold and

damp of his military base in England and then the cramped, air-less confines of a bomber. Tolley and Bubber are two young brothers who must find their way through New York City in the Depression-era novel *Cave under the City*. At the end of the book, Tolley visits his mother, who has tuberculosis and is institutional-ized in a sanatorium in upstate New York near the Canadian bor-der. Through Tolley's words, Mazer lets us know how he feels about the relative dangers of the city and the country: "I didn't like going away and leaving her again, leaving her in the moun-tains. I didn't like those cold white mountains. They say there are bears in the mountains, and wolves and mountain lions. I don't like to think about Bubber and me alone out there. I feel a lot safer in the city."[14]

A key to creating a good tale in which characters battle the environment is knowing the surroundings and portraying them convincingly. Mazer knows Canada, having lived near its border in upper New York State for most of his adult life and owning a summer camp on a lake like the one in *The Island Keeper*. He also knows the grim, windswept Tug Hill Plateau—not far from his New York home—that is the setting for *Snow Bound*. He spent the war years on the base in England and in the bomber he describes in *The Last Mission*. And New York City, the home of his childhood, is the environment that has formed him. He reminds his readers of this on the jacket flap of *Cave under the City:*

> When I was a boy, I lived and played on the streets of the city. Those were hard times, but they weren't depressing, not for us kids. We sailed boats in the gutter, chalked games on the side-walks, played ball against the walls. The street was our play-ground. Brick walls were the backstop, the frame and limit of every game.

This kind of a child's life was true for Tolley and Bubber in the opening chapters of the novel, when both their mother and their father are home in the co-ops (Workers Co-operative Colony) apartments. Their father is an unemployed house painter, and their mother works in the mills, but the boys are happy. As Tolley begins to realize that his parents are fighting more and more and that his mother is always tired, he remembers the better days, when his father would come home from work: "After he soaped himself all over he rinsed, and then he scrubbed and cleaned his fingernails and rubbed his hands raw to get the paint off. 'Take a sniff, Bubby. Do I smell?'" (13).

Reviewers of *Cave under the City* agree that one of its strengths is Mazer's development of the environment, which takes on the characteristics of a human enemy. Hugh Agee in the *ALAN Review* says that "the details of life in the city during the Depression are vivid."[15] Jim McPeak in *VOYA* agrees: "Harry Mazer brings the world of Depression-era New York City and first-generation America vividly to life in *Cave under the City*. We view this world through Tolley, and thus experience a somewhat larger than life aspect that only a 10-year-old could show us."[16] Several reviews compare Harry's development of a challenging environment with Felice Holman's portrayal of an environment with "problems needing instant decisions" in the award-winning *Slake's Limbo,* about a homeless child on the streets and under the ground in New York City.[17]

The Island Keeper places 16-year-old Cleo in a believable environment that she must conquer. Unlike Tolley and Bubber, she is on her island by choice. Fleeing from an unhappy home life, Cleo finds herself trapped there after her canoe is destroyed. The harsh winter is rapidly approaching. Mazer knows the beauty and the danger of nature, just as he knows the joys and potential horrors of the city. As suggested by a review in *Booklist,* the details in Mazer's novel not only are believable but also help build the tension. Although Cleo has spent several summers in a camp, she knows little about survival in the wild. Mazer fills the book with the beauties of an island dawn and an island sunset, swimming in the cold waters of a Canadian lake on a hot summer day, and the captivating call of an owl. But he also paints a vivid picture of cold, relentless rain and wind—a frozen world of snow, ice, and whiteness in which it is difficult to tell the sky from the lake.

Cleo, like Tolley and Bubber, also survives in a cave, but hers is a natural one. Like the boys cave under the burned-out restaurant, hers offers protection, but it also is not free from terror. The boys eventually lose their cave when its roof collapses after days of rain. Cleo discovers that her cave is cold, wet, and smoky and doesn't always offer protection from the island's wildlife.

The hostile environment in *The Last Mission* is the bomber on which Jack and the crew fly 35 missions across Europe. However, what they must conquer is not the environment itself. They must overcome the fear that comes not only from the cramped, cold plane and the other bombers they watch fall from the sky but also from the knowledge of what lies below in the smoke-filled cities of Germany:

> It wasn't the war he'd dreamed it would be back home in The Bronx. Then he'd thought he was going to be one of those flying aces zipping around the sky in a fighter plane, shooting down Germans left and right. It hadn't happened that way. He hardly thought about Hitler anymore. It was just the war, day after day, like a foot jammed in his belly. (83)

Later, after he has parachuted away from the downed plane, Jack finds himself in another hostile environment—the villages of Czechoslovakia. The injured Jack is almost captured several times—by a villager who catches him warming himself at his stove, by a cyclist who meets him as he pedals at night on a bike he has stolen from a tool shed, and by some girls who talk to him in a language he doesn't understand and then giggle and stare. Finally, after nights of running and days of hiding, Jack is caught. He is bone-tired, and he simply lets the bike take him downhill— downhill too far into a checkpoint, where a green-uniformed soldier shoots his bike from under him as he tries to escape.

After he is captured and shot, Jack is taken to a prisoner-of-war camp, where he is questioned. His dog tags are confiscated, and he feels naked; he is forced to march through town with women and girls staring at him. That night he tries to sleep on damp straw that smells of piss and mold. All night long he thinks of the downing of the plane and his dead crewmates: *"He pushed Chuckie upright. . . . Come on, Chuckie, the wing's gone. . . . They were falling through the clouds. . . . Dave was playing dead . . . the*

*wing's gone, Chuckie! Come on, Chuckie. . . . Hurry! The old
man's coming with a club. . . . Chuckie! Chuckie!"* (127).

Sympathy with the Characters

Another critical element of the survival tale is caring whether or
not the characters "make it." Readers must care about the characters as if they are real people. We care what happens to Tolley,
Bubber, Cleo, and Jack because we know them; they are like us
and like our friends. They have authentic voices, and this is very
important to Mazer, who is "very strongly connected with the
voice of the character."

In *Cave under the City,* Tolley is a typical 10-year-old. And, like
most boys his age, he both loves and resents his little brother.
Even at the beginning of the novel, he hates having to care for
Bubber and having his little brother follow him everywhere.
Sometimes he even loses Bubber, but then he feels guilty. When
the boys are on their own, Tolley is fiercely protective of the 5-
year-old; but at that same time, he tires of the younger boy's
incessant questioning, crying, and hunger:

> "Is that a lot of money?" Bubber asked.
> "Do you have to know the price of everything?"
> "How much?"
> "Two times seven cents."
> "Fourteen."
> "Plus a nickel for the soda."
> "Nineteen. Is that a lot of money?"
> "What do you think?" (51–52)

We care about Tolley and Bubber because they are real people.
Tolley is forced to steal in order to feed his sick brother and himself, but he feels guilty and vows to someday repay Mr. Lazinski
for the stolen jelly donuts. At the end of the novel, when he is
again home with his father and has a newspaper route, he gives
the milkman—from whom he had stolen milk—a free newspaper
each day. Tolley, like all of us, has mixed emotions. He loves and

hates his little brother; he is protective of him but at the same time cannot really accept the adult responsibility of being a parent. One day, after a typical boys' argument, Tolley leaves Bubber and the mutt Bubber has named King in front of a movie theater, and he goes off by himself to gaze at the river. When he suddenly realizes that he has deserted his brother and may never be able to find him again, he runs as fast as he can back to where he last saw him. Bubber, fortunately, remained with King on the curb where Tolley had left them.

And Bubber, too, is a real human being. Mazer is able to give this first-grader endearing qualities. He is like all young children—fearful of being left alone, and playful. He asks incessant questions, cries when he is frustrated, and wants to be loved. Bubber is also a child of contradictions. Tolley reports that he is not very good at reading and does not do well in school. He can't remember letters and sounds and gets angry when Tolley tries to teach him. But numbers are obviously another story; Bubber can add, subtract, and do simple multiplication—quite a task for a first-grader. He is also the one who is able to make an adult decision when Tolley falls ill, the cave has been destroyed, and they have nowhere to go:

> Bubber shook me. "Tolley!" He pulled me to my feet. "We're going home."
> "We can't. . . . You can't. . . ." I knocked into him. I was rolling around. I couldn't stay on my feet. "McKenzie's there."
> "If we see him we'll run away." Bubber took me home. (142)

We also like Cleo in *The Island Keeper*. Although she has lived a rich and privileged childhood, she has suffered great pain and loss. Throughout her childhood years, her younger sister, Jam, continuously asks Cleo to tell her about their mother and what happened on the day she was killed:

> "What I remember, Jam, is the horse. His head came through the windshield. It was a runaway. I don't remember being thrown from the car. It was winter. It was snowing. A lot of snow. Mother was sitting on the ground. Blood was coming out

of her mouth. She was moving her hands, trying to speak, and
someone was screaming."

   "That was me."

   "Yes. You were screaming. That's all I remember." (10)

After the death of their mother, Cleo and Jam live with their
grandmother, who is old-fashioned and doesn't understand young
girls, and with their father, who is usually away on business.
However, most of their time is spent away at boarding schools
and camps:

> Cleo had been sent away to school when she was eight. Jam,
> who was four years younger, stayed home till she was seven,
> then she, too, was sent away. Different schools, different camps.
> Her grandmother chose them all, but after a while she always
> found something wrong. In eight years—she was sixteen now—
> Cleo had attended four different schools. It became harder and
> harder to make friends. She was forever packing and unpacking,
> coming and going, or getting ready to go. (3)

The previous summer Cleo and Jam had again been sent to different camps. Cleo's camp was selected to help her deal with her
weight problem, and that's where she learned of the death of her
sister: "Only a week later the call came from her grandmother.
Cleo took it in the barn, where she had been saddling up a horse
for one of the younger girls. 'Cleo? Something's happened.
There's been an accident . . . a terrible accident'" (16).

   Jam had been in a boat on the lake alone. The water was
choppy. Although no one knew for sure what had happened, she
had drowned, tangled in the ropes of the boat. And this summer
Cleo was facing going back to the same camp again. It was a sce-
nario she could not bear, and so she imagines how she will run
away to Duke Island, a place she and Jam had loved in their childhood.

   If we are to feel concern for the characters, suspense must
build. One of the best ways to create suspense is by allowing the
reader to feel that "this could be me." *Cave under the City* is "well
told in Tolley's believably adolescent voice."[18] *The Island Keeper*

is clearly in Cleo's voice, but it is told by a third-person narrator, which allows us to see dangers Cleo does not herself recognize. Perhaps for this reason reviewers have found it less convincing. According to Lorraine Douglas in a *School Library Journal* review, "The story of Cleo's past is told in imaginary scenes and conversations with her family, the effect of which seems stilted and artificial and adds no real conflict."[19]

We also care about Jack in *The Last Mission,* because we have experienced the pain of war with him. We know how he feels when he sees the back of Chuckie's head blown off. We understand why he wants to believe that Dave is playing dead as he watches his parachute fall to the ground. We understand Jack's anger and fear as he tells Stan he's a Jew. We can feel his terror as he realizes the Germans have seen the *H* on his dog tag, which identifies him as Jewish (Hebrew). We, too, shiver when he enters the showers in the German hospital, wondering if he will share the fate of the Jews in the concentration camps. We care what happens to Jack because he's only 16, and we have grown up with him from the young boy afraid to call Dotty on the phone to the man who rides a bike by night to escape from his captors. We empathize with him when he sees a German boy without legs being pulled in a wooden wagon. "All those bombs they had dropped—he had never thought they would be blowing kids away" (142). We know that Jack is real when he can think these thoughts as he is being marched day after day through the streets of Czechoslovakia. We understand Jack's resistance to giving another young boy his egg; Jack is hungry, he's been marching for days, and he sees the boy as "some little Jew hater who'd swallowed Hitler's crap with his baby food" (144). We understand that it is easy to hate, but we are not surprised that Jack can't eat the egg and holds it out to share with the boy. We also understand Jack's smile when the boy rolls a cigarette, takes a puff, and then gives it to Jack. We care about Jack. He is real; he is angry; he is frightened; he is kind; he wants to go on living; he wants to forget.

The Resolution

In all survival tales there must be a resolution, and this is particularly true of young adult books. Readers must believe that the characters can and will survive; they must believe that they, too, can survive. According to Carolyn W. Carmichael, Harry Mazer's "stories are stories of feeling, crisis, and resolution. The nightmares, the fearful journeys, the testings can be lived vicariously through the characters, and readers, by identification, can begin to sense and believe in their own strength."[20] Mazer's characters have grit, intelligence, and strength. They not only survive their ordeals but most often can look forward to a life made better by them. There is no doubt that Cleo has grown through her experiences on the island. She is no longer fat; she is no longer afraid; she can survive her own isolation and loneliness. Tony, too, in *Snow Bound* has overcome his environment and his own fears. He has come to learn the importance of others in his life.

The resolution in *The Last Mission* does not represent the end of Jack's pain and fear. We know that he will never forget his friend Chuckie's death, just as Mazer continues to have questions about Mike Brennan's death. We know that it will be years before he can begin to answer such questions as why he lived when his crewmates died and why they flew that last mission when the war was almost over. However, we also know that he is beginning to understand how he has changed. And he is beginning to understand that the memories of his friends' deaths will live with him the rest of his life, just as Mazer's own war has lived with him.

6. Romantic Fiction
for Male Readers

"A romantic who dreamed of becoming a writer, posed as a musician, and dreamed of girls." That might be a good way to sum up the
adolescent Harry Mazer. His dreams of girls went completely unfulfilled. According to Mazer, he and his friends were the kind who
looked at girls but did not go after them. Most of the way through an
all-male high school and college, he had no relationships or even
friendships with girls. He didn't know how to talk to them.

Mazer was sometimes taunted by girls as a teenager. He was
shy and only looked at them when he thought they were not looking. Unlike the popular athletes in his classes, he was smart and
didn't dress in the latest styles. He was also overweight and
looked silly on the playground when he tried to boost himself up
on the monkey bars. He often looked longingly after girls and
heard them giggling and sneering at him as he passed them on
the street. When he was near girls he held his head high up in the
air, not looking at them.

Perhaps because of these difficulties during his adolescence,
Mazer often writes romantic fiction for male readers. Although
his books do not contain messages, they do tell boys that you are
not alone—that other boys have similar problems. Like Marcus
and Willis, you will grow beyond the awkward stage and will meet
girls with whom you can talk and have relationships.

In Mazer's romances, the boys' relationships with girls and
women are often thwarted. The boys do not understand how to
talk to girls, do not know that relationships go far beyond sex.
Mazer's romance novels are far more complex than most young

adult romances. They are more than romances, recognizing that adolescents are not one-dimensional and must deal with many aspects of growing up at the same time. Mazer's romances are realistic coming-of-age books in which relationships and developing sexuality are critical to the protagonist's development. In these novels, the male protagonists learn about themselves and grow in and out of their romantic and sexual relationships.

The Male Perspective

One of the things that sets Mazer's romances apart from most young adult romances is that they have male romantic protagonists. Although his books are and should be read by both male and female readers, they are primarily told from the male perspective. At the same time, they successfully incorporate the female's perspective—sometimes shifting point of view between chapters. One of the major strengths of Mazer's books are that his female romantic figures are every bit as strong as his male romantic figures. Often, in fact, they are emotionally stronger than their male partners.

Mazer's romances have authentic characters that we recognize as real people with real problems. We don't always like them, but we always care about them. They have human voices and real feelings. They get angry, and they make us angry. They cry, and we cry with them. We know these people. In fact, they are us.

Mazer, unlike some teenage romance authors, does not avoid issues of developing sexuality. In fact, Marcus's sexual development is one of two major issues in *I Love You, Stupid!* It is not the only issue Marcus faces, but it is important for his developing maturity. Mazer deals with Marcus's sexual development with humor, guilt, honesty, and integrity. Sexuality is a central aspect of the coming of age of all adolescents, so it is essential that it be dealt with sensitively in young adult fiction.

Of Mazer's 13 individually written novels, 4 can be classified as young adult romances: *The Girl of His Dreams, Hey, Kid! Does She Love Me? City Light,* and *I Love You, Stupid!*

There is no doubt that *The Girl of His Dreams* falls into the genre of romantic fiction for young adults. Almost every reviewer talks about it is as a love story or a romance. In this novel, Mazer writes of the romance of two ordinary young people with, according to Marianne Gingher in the *Los Angeles Times,* "a credibility apart from its fairy-tale ending." Because these characters are "dimensional . . . the happy ending feels earned. . . . *The Girl of His Dreams* is mostly, undeniably, a love story. Gradually we see the loosening in Willis. His heart unclenches. . . . [H]e begins to notice when Sophie isn't around. He misses her terribly when they've argued and separated. Ironically their arguments bring them closer and create the necessary mystery between them, the sense of 'otherness' that inspires love."[1]

In spite of its title, *The Girl of His Dreams* is not a typical romance in which the boy gets the girl. Without doubt, Willis is a dreamer; he dreams not only of a beautiful girl but also of becoming a famous runner. Sophie Brown is definitely not the girl of his dreams. However, it is Sophie who helps him learn that dreams may be important, but they are only dreams until we turn them into something real. *The Girl of His Dreams* is neither a fairy tale nor a clichéd romance. Instead it is populated with real, multidimensional characters with real problems that go far beyond their romantic interests.

Hey, Kid! Does She Love Me? is an unusual romance, not at all like the fairy-tale romances of formula fiction in which the girl gets the boy, loses the boy, and finds the boy again. Jeff Orloff is not a typical romantic hero; he is a dishwasher who does not know what he wants to do with his life. He is a dreamer who dreams of directing films in Hollywood and tells much of his story as though it were a movie script. This allows Mazer to write these passages in the first person—from inside Jeff's head—but at the same time to keep the benefits of telling the story in the third person: *"Fade in:* Mary looks out her window, sees Jeff. Puzzled, but intrigued. *Cut to Jeff:* A look of recognition. *Quick cuts:* Mary at window. Jeff on sidewalk. Lines flowing between them, a whole net of lines, the two of them caught and tangled in an understanding truer than words. *Music up"* (25).

Jeff falls in love with Mary Silver, an older girl he remembers from high school. She, too, is not a typical romantic heroine, but a 20-year-old with a baby girl, Hannah, whom she neither wanted nor knows how to care for. Jeff pursues Mary, even baby-sitting for Hannah for several days while Mary goes to acting school. The romance does not have a "they lived happily ever after" ending. Mary decides to leave Jeff and join an acting commune, and Jeff struggles in California as a studio kitchen worker and gofer who takes acting classes in hopes of breaking into the movies.

City Light is also an unlikely romance. It is the story of high school senior George Farina's life after Julie, his girlfriend of many years, dumps him. Unlike the hero of a formula romance, George loses one girl and finds another girl, but he is not sure he wants to spend his entire life with either of them. George, like Mazer's other romantic heroes, is also searching for what he wants to do with his life. This search is complicated because George's father wants him to take over the family business, but George wants to find his own way.

I Love You, Stupid! is probably the most controversial of Mazer's books. Most criticism has focused on the sex in the book rather than on the romance. Although Mazer admits that *I Love You, Stupid!* is undeniably about sex, it is also about an authentic relationship between Marcus, who dreams of being a writer, and Wendy, who reenters Marcus's life after several years. He had known her as the weird kid whose mother was his mother's best friend in *The Dollar Man*. Although Marcus is preoccupied with thoughts of sex throughout this second novel about him, Wendy teaches him that there is more to a relationship than sex. It is not until he nearly loses her because of his preoccupation and insensitivity that he learns that caring and concern are important elements of any relationship:

> "Look, I don't want to fight. I just came over to say good-bye. We set out to do something, we did it. I thought it was good. You didn't." He put up his hands. "So be it."
> "It didn't have to end this way," she said. "It was good in the beginning, but you didn't care about my feelings."

"Feelings!" he exclaimed. "What do you know about feelings? You don't know anything, you don't see anything. I'm trying to tell you something." He spun around and walked away.

"Well, say it," she called after him. "What? What?"

He turned and looked her right in the eye. He could have hit her, she was so thick. "I love you, stupid!" (182–83)

Sex in Mazer's Romances

According to Harry Mazer, *I Love You, Stupid!* is "unashamedly about sex. . . . It's about sexual curiosity, the need, the frustration. It's about two kids' first sexual relationship. It's also about relationships and how sex and feelings are intertwined. How sex, without friendship, without love, destroys itself" (Illinois Librarians). Marcus is preoccupied with thoughts of having sex. He dreams of it with almost every girl he meets. He believes there is something wrong with him because he has not yet had sex:

> He came back to earth, aware of the antiseptic smell, the warmth, the slackness in his belly. Out of bed, muttering to himself, he changed everything. Seventeen, and still jerking off like a maniac. He wasn't proud of it. Procrastinator. Masturbator. Everything wrong with him had a Latin name, like a disease. Couldn't get a girl. What was the Latin word for that? (37)

When Marcus meets Wendy, a girl he had known in *The Dollar Man,* and goes to her home, the first thing he does is jump on top of her. She throws him off; he apologizes, and, in spite of his foolish actions, they become friends. He tells Wendy of his dreams of Karen, the beautiful mother of the young boy he baby-sits for each day. Eventually convincing himself that Karen is interested in him, he attempts to kiss her. She fires him, and he is devastated.

Wendy feels sorry for Marcus, and he finally convinces her that since they are friends, they should have sex with each other. This way they can both climb the wall together—the wall separating childhood from adulthood. Marcus writes of his pact with Wendy:

After a period of round-the-clock negotiations, Marcus Rosenbloom and Wendy Barrett have reached an agreement on a delicate subject, the agreement to be implemented in an as-yet-
undesignated location, sometime soon. The two young people
have no one else to do it with, are tired of waiting for it to happen, and know they can trust each other not to be moody, ugly,
exploitive, or sensational about the upcoming event. (121)

Their first attempts at physical intimacy are awkward and
involve only kissing and petting. Finally, they have sex for the
first time:

> "Marcus, do you think anybody's as slow and ignorant as we
> are?"
> "I doubt it, but we'll get it." They kissed again, touched and
> kissed, and rolled around the bed. His breath was coming short.
> He fumbled, excited and scared. "Wendy, are you all right? . . .
> Should I? . . . Is it all right?" (144)

After they initially make love, they are still awkward in their
attempts, often not finding a place to be alone together. Wendy
begins to think that the only thing Marcus wants from her is
sex—that he doesn't care about her beyond their sexual relationship. She runs from him and tells him she doesn't want to see him
again. After this, Marcus gradually begins to realize that he has
been selfish and that he really cares for Wendy.

Hey, Kid! Does She Love Me? is not directly about sex. However, as one reviewer suggests, Jeff is "alternately starry-eyed
and horny (a condition he describes with some vivid slang)."[2] One
day Mary and Jeff go to the lake to talk. Jeff is playing guide,
pointing out sights, but he is thinking other thoughts:

> He pointed, he moved his arm, he knelt down next to her. The
> Guide. The Professor of Fruit and Passion. She'd pulled the
> shift up over her knees. He drew a leaf of grass lightly over her
> bare leg. He leaned toward her. Kiss? Was she in the mood? He
> had the need to touch her, to lie down next to her and put his
> arms around her and press himself against her. . . .
> I'm on my knees next to you. In a prayerful position. I bow
> down to you. I am wild for you. My heart and my prick, I offer

them both to you. I worship your knees. I want you to raise your shift, pull it over your head. Are you wearing anything underneath? We're alone (except for the baby). I kick off my sneakers for you. My feet are bare for you. Look how I wiggle my toes invitingly. Don't you think I'm sexy? If you take off your clothes, I'll take off mine. (93)

On the other hand, *The Girl of His Dreams* is "romantic without being either mushy or explicitly sexual. Willis and Sophie are attractive characters. . . . Friends and lovers, they grow in trust and maturity page by page."[3] Mazer devotes a chapter to Willis's thinking about making love to Sophie. Perhaps out of embarrassment or guilt, Willis removes himself from his thought process by thinking about the act in the second person. "Up in Sophie's place, you get some definite ideas. You've had them before, in the pool and in the car, but never as strongly as now" (*Girl,* 126). The chapter is not explicit, and yet we understand Willis's thoughts clearly: "And she lies against you, and all she wants to do is cuddle and get close, but her bare skin is like nothing you've ever known, and there are tears in your eyes, because it's more than you can contain, and you just hug her and hang on her and say, Damn" (130). Reviewer Zena Sutherland says of this book, it is "a love story that's sweet without being sugary, original without being outlandish, sophisticated without being outré."[4]

One of the important themes of Mazer's romances is that love relationships require more than sex. It is essential that the relationship grow in many ways—that the partners care about each other's feelings, that they respect each other, and that they work together to help each other achieve their dreams. The books also make it clear that no matter how much a person cares about another, sometimes the relationship must wait, and maybe it will not grow beyond initial longings. All of Mazer's romances are primarily coming-of-age books in which the characters are growing in many directions and only secondarily romances in which the characters are learning that through relationships we understand more about ourselves. The characters in his novels are searching for themselves both in and out of romantic and sexual relationships. For this reason, Mazer's romances are important reading for both young males and young females.

Romance, Sex, and Censorship

It is almost impossible to write young adult fiction about sex and not experience the wrath of censors. Although many of Mazer's books have been attacked, the most frequent target is *I Love You, Stupid!* Mazer says that the book has a message: that sex without love and friendship destroys itself. However, a novel is not a place to preach. A novel "shows life . . . demonstrates life" (Illinois Librarians).

Although Mazer does not fail to show life in his novels, he does temper life to keep the books on the shelves of libraries and classrooms. A good example of this is the language in *The Last Mission*. Since this book is largely autobiographical, Mazer knows that the language of the young men placed in life-and-death situations would be far more graphic than what appears on the pages of his book. Although he uses some expletives, he replaces others with milder language. He is willing to do this so that his books are more readily available to young readers, but he will not alter a book so that it no longer paints a true picture of life. "The writer has to tell the truth as he knows it. Otherwise, the world he creates will be false" (Illinois Librarians). The sources and inspirations for Mazer's books are his "experiences, thoughts, and feelings" (interview with author). The stories he tells of the sexual frustrations of Marcus, Willis, George, and Jeff are the truth as Mazer knows it—the truth from his own life. That is why his characters are authentic, his stories real, and his books important.

Empathetic Characters

One of the distinguishing features of good romances for young adults is characters that readers care about—characters with whom we can empathize. Mazer's romances are filled with authentic characters—characters who are not unlike the way he was as an adolescent and who are not unlike the way we were and are. Mazer's characters struggle with many things. They have problems not only within their romantic relationships but also at home, at school, and at work. They are searching to find how best to live their lives. Often they are frustrated; they make mistakes.

The Girl of His Dreams is an appealing romance because Willis Pierce, although not always likable, is an appealing character. Willis, whom we met previously in *The War on Villa Street,* is a runner. The book begins: "He ran. The night flowed past him. No thoughts, no words, no need for words. The air flowing through him. Fluid, like water. Like music. Exactly like music. Thoughts brushed aside. Only the wind in his ears, the light drag of his breath and the steady tap of his feet" (1). But Willis is not a runner who wins races; he is merely a boy who runs.

Willis is also a loner, an 18-year-old living alone in the city. His parents have moved south because of his father's heart. Willis works in a factory, in shipping, and dreams of finding a girl. Willis's workplace is one that Harry knows well. It is a factory near where he lived and worked for several years, but he could not get a job there because of his politics.

Willis has an idol. His name is Aaron Hill, and he is a runner, a college boy. Willis wants to be like Aaron, but he has run competitively only once. After that race, his father embarrassed him by blundering onto the track drunk. That happened when Willis was in eighth grade. After that, Willis quit running in competition. College is out of the question for him. One day Willis finds a dog in a bag with her hind legs tied together. She is a puppy, nearly dead. He takes her home, puts her in the tub, and gives her water. Willis names her Zola after Zola Budd, the South African runner who was well known for running in her bare feet.

The story shifts to Sophie Brown, a 22-year-old farm girl who has been living with her brother, sister-in-law, and two children. Sophie works the farm and takes care of the children. Pat, her sister-in-law, is pregnant again and tells Sophie there will not be room for her in the house; they'll build her a room in the garage.

Sophie knows she's in the way and decides to leave. She gets on
the bus and goes to the city. She knows no one but meets Brenda
in the grocery store just after she arrives. Brenda tells her that
there is a dirty apartment in her building. If Sophie is willing to
clean it up, she is sure the landlord will give her a good deal on it.
Sophie gets a job running the newspaper stand near the factory at
which Willis works. She sees Willis on the first day and is smitten,
but he does not notice her for some time. Sophie is plain, a country girl without makeup, not at all the girl of Willis's dreams—not
at all the beautiful girl of the typical young adult romance. Sophie
is a real person, the kind of girl we all know.

We also care about the characters in Harry's other romances.
Marcus's sexual frustration and inept attempts at developing
relationships in *I Love You, Stupid!* make him a sympathetic
character. His preoccupation with the sex act is not offensive;
rather it is humorous and sad. He is so preoccupied with his vir-
ginal state that he has difficulty functioning in any relationship
with a female. His ineptitude is real and understandable. Wendy
is also a likable character. She is a good friend to Marcus—perhaps too good a friend. She is more mature than he, and she
understands his problems. However, she seems to be more aware
of Marcus's problems than she is of her own problems and needs.
Her pact with Marcus on a "delicate subject" almost destroys
their relationship.

Although George Farina is annoyingly possessive in *City Light,*
his feelings toward Julie and her avoidance of him make him a
sympathetic character. He and Julie had their entire lives planned;
it was so easy. George knew he and Julie would live happily ever
after. But life is not a fairy tale. Julie is growing beyond George;
she wants something more from life. George is crushed, but when
he meets Rosemary, he learns that there are other girls in the
world. He still thinks about Julie, but he comes to recognize that
Rosemary is helping him learn new things about himself:

> "Sing to me," she said.
> I started singing some old corny song. *"On top of old
> Smokeeee. . . ."*

"Nice," she murmured and sang with me.
Julie and I never sang. I didn't even know I could sing. (175)

Jeff Orloff in *Hey, Kid! Does She Love Me?* is also a real person with unrealized dreams. He has just graduated from high school, and he doesn't know what do to with his life. His family (parents, older sister, and brother) think he should go to college. He wants to save money to go to California to get a job in the movies. When the novel begins, he is painting his parents' house and working as a dishwasher.

Jeff is not a particularly likable character. As one reviewer suggests in *Booklist,* he is "too selfish and too self-involved."[5] However, we can't help but sympathize with him when he ineptly attempts to take care of the baby, Hannah, so that Mary can attend an acting workshop—even if his motives are questionable and his original plan is selfish. He had volunteered to have his mother care for Hannah, forgetting to ask her until 2 days before Mary is to leave. When he finally does ask his mother, she reminds him that she and his father will be at his sister's wedding. His selfishness is almost humorous when he asks why his mother can't change the date of the wedding—after all, it's too late and too hard to ask Mary to change her plans. Of course, his volunteering to care for Hannah is a ploy to win Mary's heart, but his clumsy attempts at caring for the baby when he's left with no other choice are honest and heartwarming.

Unrequited Romance

All of the major characters in Mazer's romances are atypical romantic heroes and heroines. Not one of them is a heartthrob; not one is particularly popular; there are no football heroes and no cheerleaders among them. They are not rich and must work for a living. They have dreams, but often their dreams are thwarted by circumstance. There are no Prince Charmings and no princesses on whom to place the glass slipper. Mazer's romances are not fairy tales; often they are one-sided, and always they are awkward. There are no fairy-tale heroes or heroines in his novels. And the resolutions are open-ended: We are never convinced that the characters will live "happily ever after."

Marcus in *I Love You, Stupid!* has grown from a fat kid into a rather good-looking high school senior. Despite his handsomeness and his preoccupation with girls, the girls do not return his interest. Marcus is a dreamer who frequently lives in another world—the world of a writer. When he is unable to force himself actually to write, he gets a job as a baby-sitter and is fascinated with Karen, the mother of the little boy he is watching. His preoccupation with sex and with himself leads him to mistake Karen's friendliness and concern for romantic interest in him. He loses his job after he attempts to kiss her.

Willis in *The Girl of His Dreams* is not much better at knowing how to relate to girls. One day the wind blows the shutter of the newsstand down on Sophie's hand. Willis is walking by, and he runs to a nearby diner for a first-aid kit and treats her injury. However, he shows no interest in Sophie beyond helping her. He is still searching for the girl of his dreams. He goes on a blind date with Benny, his friend from work, with Benny's beautiful girlfriend Lee, and with Lee's friend Dore. Dore, Willis's date, is pretty, but Lee is a knockout. The date is a disaster, much like the blind date Mazer remembers having when he was in basic training in Miami. When Willis arrives home, Zola, his new puppy, shows more enthusiasm for him in 5 minutes than he had from Dore the entire evening.

Willis goes to the food market where Dore and Lee work in hopes of seeing Lee. He sees Dore, but she does not see him. While there, he also runs into Sophie, but he does not remember her name. He thinks of her as smiling too much and being too eager and too naive.

Sophie recognizes that she likes Willis too much and that she is not being cool. One day Sophie brings Willis cookies. He does not want to take them, but he invites her in and then teases her about liking to fly a plane—Sophie dreams of becoming a pilot. She is hurt:

> "No, I mean, are you going to be something? A crop duster?"
> "Are you going to be a messenger boy, Willis?" (76)

Willis suddenly realizes that he likes Sophie, that he likes looking at her. He sees Sophie in the park. A relationship—not one of his dreams but maybe one of reality—is beginning to develop.

Jeff Orloff and Mary Silver in *Hey, Kid! Does She Love Me?* have a romance that lives primarily in Jeff's inner life. To Mary, Jeff is merely a friend who helps her out with her baby, Hannah. But to Jeff, Mary is the girl he has dreamed of. Jeff's images of himself with Mary are sexual and romantic. He sees himself married to her and making love to her. Mary, in many ways, uses Jeff's infatuation to help her through a difficult time in her life. She recognizes his infatuation, doesn't return it, tells him she only wants to be friends, but doesn't send him away. Mary needs Jeff as much as he needs her, but for very different reasons. At one point, Mary unconvincingly attempts to tell Jeff that she wants to be just friends, but he doesn't hear her: "'Oh, Jeff! Why can't you stay on the level? Your friendship means a lot to me. I don't want to lose that. But it's got to be like you said. Friends, like in friends, friends, friends'" (95).

Although Jeff keeps dreaming and plotting to make his relationship with Mary more than a friendship, it never grows. At the end of the novel, Jeff writes to Mary from California:

> I think about us, sometimes. I feel like I was really young then. I tried to make everything so simple, tried to pretend we were just a boy and a girl. No connections. No Hannah, no families, just us and our dreams and desires, or should I say, Just me and my dreams and my desires. I wanted Mary. All I wanted was Mary. No, that's not true. I always wanted more.
>
> What I'm trying to say is, right now I'm glad I'm in California and you're in Massachusetts. You're on the Atlantic and I'm on the Pacific and we're both doing what we want to do. Getting closer to what we want. (185)

Relationships That Grow?

Harry Mazer knows from experience that developing relationships is not easy. In real life and in realistic romance novels, the relationships may grow, but not without a struggle. The characters, like most adolescents, are self-absorbed and consumed by their own problems, longings, and frustrations. In order for the relationship to develop, each of them must learn to care about the other as much as about himself or herself. Only if the characters can do this will the fictional relationship grow. Because all of Mazer's characters are adolescents, the jury is still out on whether they will be able to develop beyond self-absorption. Realistically, then, each of his novels has an open-ended conclusion in which the reader is not sure the relationship will continue to mature along with the adolescent protagonists.

From tentative beginnings, the relationship between Willis and Sophie grows in *The Girl of His Dreams*. Willis, however, is not always sure that he wants to give up the girl of his dreams for Sophie, and his foolish actions almost cause him to lose her. Sophie, on the other hand, wants to help Willis accomplish his dream of becoming a runner. She has not yet focused on her own dreams and will have to do so if their relationship is to strengthen. They talk about Aaron Hill, who will run in the college track meet in June. Willis begins to train as though he can run in the meet despite the fact that he is not a student at the college and is not on the team. He goes to the college track one day, and the coach thinks that he's a freshman. He says to Willis, "I like the way you run. You want to let it go to waste, that's your business, but if you get out here every day, I can make a runner out of you" (150).

At first Willis is elated, but something happens when he and Sophie go to swim. He thinks he sees Lee, the girl he has been dreaming about, on the diving platform. He begins to question his life: "Was this all people did? Work and sleep and eat and eat and eat some more?" (154). Like many young people, he mixes up one set of dreams with another. He thinks he wants more from his life, and this includes wanting more than Sophie. Suddenly he is shaken back into reality. "Famous? Race Aaron Hill? He was a dreamer, and that made him a fool" (154). He decides to stop going to the coach's practices.

Willis gives up training, but he does not tell Sophie. One day at the zoo, they run into Benny and Lee. Lee asks Willis about his running, and Sophie tells her he runs every day. Willis gets angry.

Benny wants Lee to sit on a camel. When the camel begins to walk about, the pony boy does not chase after him. Sophie recognizes that the boy knows the camel will not run, but Willis goes to rescue Lee. Sophie sees the look in his eyes as Willis helps Lee, and she realizes that he is smitten by Lee.

Sophie runs away, but Willis finds her and follows her on the bus, leaving his car at the zoo. Sophie suggests they go their own ways. Willis does not see Sophie except when he passes the newsstand, but one day she is not there. Brenda tells him that Sophie has gone back to the farm. He begins to realize he loves her. "It was like the music. Before you heard it, everything was ordinary. Then you heard the music and you went toward it and you saw the players and people dancing and you felt like dancing and you were happy and you thought the music would never stop. And then it did" (173).

Willis begins running again—better than ever. He begins training to race against Aaron Hill. He thinks Sophie will come to the race, and he must be there. The morning of the race, he goes to the arena in his warm-up clothes and waits for the 1,500-meter race. When they announce it, he takes off his warm-up suit, puts on his track shoes, and enters the track as if he were from one of the schools. He has the number 19, his age now, on his back. He begins the race just after the other runners. The officials realize that he is not a student, and they try to remove him from the race. Willis runs his heart out and beats every runner except Hill—and almost beats him, too.

The relationship between Marcus and Wendy in *I Love You, Stupid!* is fraught with difficulties. It begins tentatively as a friendship after Marcus's mistake about Wendy's interest in him. Marcus finds himself jealous that his friend Wendy is interested in his friend Alec, whom he sees as the master of conquests. Their friendship continues as Marcus tells Wendy of his feelings for Karen. Because they are friends, Marcus and Wendy agree to become adults together by making love. However, after they have made love several times, Wendy feels that Marcus is not interested in her or in what she thinks; he seems to be interested only in sex. Wendy tells Marcus to leave her alone:

"Don't. *Don't.* Just leave me alone. I don't want to be pawed, Marcus. You don't own me."

"I never said I did."

"But that's what you think."

He couldn't get things straight. Whatever he said only made it worse. It was like falling down a slippery chute, going down and down. He couldn't stop himself.

"You don't care about me," she said. "It's just lie down! Every time you come around—Lie down!" She jumped up, left him there on the hill, and ran back to the beach. By the time he came down she was gone, and so was her bike. (163)

Almost Fairy Tales?

Although Harry Mazer's romances are not fairy tales, they do have some of the literary elements of the form. There are unlikely heroes who often get the girl despite being convinced that they won't. There are almost-miraculous occurrences. And, most definitely, there is the romantic quest of the romantic hero.

As one reviewer suggests, "contrivances abound in [*The Girl of His Dreams*], the way they do in fairy tales, but the happy ending feels earned."[6] After the race, Willis is pulled back into the locker room, but the college officials decide to let him go. Would this have occurred in real life? The next day, there is an article in the paper. Later a reporter comes to see him and writes an article about his running. He is a hero at work, but Sophie was not at the race, and all he can do is think of her. The dean from the college, who is angry about what Willis did, calls and asks him to come to his office. Two other men are there, and one is the track coach. The dean lets Willis know that what he did was dangerous. They ask him what kind of student he was in high school, and they offer him a scholarship—another miraculous event.

The article in the paper makes him infamous at work, but his notoriety soon begins to fade. He wants to see Sophie and imagines writing a personal ad in the newspaper to her. One day he begins driving aimlessly; soon he realizes he is going to see Sophie. His car breaks down, and he and Zola walk the rest of the way. They find Sophie working near the barn in the rain. They wait out the storm inside the barn, and Sophie tells Willis she was waiting for him to come:

> He was still Willis Pierce, but he was different.
> He'd done something that he'd never thought he could do. He'd proved something to himself. He could change. He'd run the race, he'd run against Aaron Hill. He'd done something he'd dreamed of and been afraid of. He'd done it to prove to her that he didn't have to be the way he was, that he could do something else, be somebody else. (207)

Sophie comes back to the city, and Willis suggests that they live together so he can save money. Willis has still not grown beyond the self-centered adolescent stage. When she refuses, he argues at first but finally realizes that he is being selfish: "Being close with someone isn't easy, he thinks. It's not just a matter of saying I love you. When you're with somebody else, when you like that person and love that person, you have to think about them as much as you think about yourself" (214). Although this is not exactly a fairy-tale ending—since we are not sure whether the relationship will continue to grow—the novel does end happily. However, there will be difficult times ahead. Willis and Sophie will struggle. As one reviewer suggests, Sophie "is willing to love but not settle for less than equality."[7] She is not a typical fairy-tale heroine. And if their relationship is to grow, Willis will have to become less selfish and work not only to reach his own dreams but also to help Sophie achieve hers.

In *The Dollar Man,* Marcus's Uncle Albert tells him: "Fairy tales contain the wisdom of the ages. . . . Every young man has to run away from home—the sooner the better."[8] Marcus in *I Love You, Stupid!* does not run away from home like a character in a fairy tale, but he strikes out on his own. He leaves school each afternoon in an attempt to become a writer. When he is less than successful, he seeks a baby-sitting job. Sally, his mother, complains that Marcus doesn't talk to her any more—doesn't tell her what he is thinking. Marcus, like the heroes of all fairy tales, is finding his own way. Sally helps him along by keeping him from stumbling too badly, and Wendy does the same; but Marcus is primarily on his own.

The romance between Marcus and Wendy is far from a fairy-tale romance, however. It is tentative and awkward. Although the book ends on a positive note, with Marcus learning that love is more important in a relationship than sex, we are not sure whether this relationship will continue. There is no fairy-tale, happily-ever-after ending here.

Even further from the typical fairy-tale ending is *Hey, Kid! Does She Love Me?* Jeff Orloff does not get the girl he dreams of. Instead he goes to California in quest of another dream—a romantic quest. By the end of the novel, he realizes that his relationship with Mary was not meant to be, that right now they are both better off pursuing their own dreams independently. Someday, he hopes, they will meet again; someday the fairy tale will resume. "But we're going to meet again. One of these months or years, the east will meet the west. What a reunion it will be" (185).

In many fairy tales, there are unlikely heroes. This is true in Mazer's romances as well. Willis in *The Girl of His Dreams* is a runner and a loner. He works in a factory but goes to run on the college track; someone is running behind him, nipping at his heels. Is it Aaron Hill, his hero, the college runner? When Willis turns around, no one is there; but then he sees a figure disappearing behind the fence. Sophie—the plain, older girl who works at a newspaper stand—begins to help Willis train. They have a big fight when Carl, Sophie's boss, runs into them at the diner and Willis is jealous because Sophie seems to be paying more attention to Carl than to him. Willis leaves the diner. He realizes that he doesn't want to be without Sophie, and they make up. Willis and Sophie are both unlikely romantic heroes.

Jeff in *Hey, Kid! Does She Love Me?* sees himself as a great hero of the silver screen. Much of his life is lived through the movie scripts he concocts within his head. However, in real life he is a high school graduate working as a dishwasher and a painter—not exactly the typical princely hero. However, like the characters of fairy tales, he turns into an unwilling prince by taking care of Mary's baby while she attends an acting workshop. Little does he realize that this gesture will not gain him his princess, but it will take her off to a new career in acting.

Although some of the elements of the fairy tale are present in Mazer's novels, as they are in all romances, these books are realistic romances, the stories of real people. Frequently the hero does not win the heroine, or at least not in the way he expected. The books, however, always end on a positive note—the hero has grown beyond the romance or in the romance. He has learned that sex is not all there is to a romantic relationship and that sometimes separating is the only way the two people can achieve their goals.

Links among Novels

An intriguing aspect of Mazer's work is that many of the books connect with other books through characters, settings, and plot elements. Some of the connections are obvious. Two of Mazer's romances have the same protagonists as earlier novels. In this way, he can continue the coming-of-age saga beyond a single book.

Other connections are less obvious and are only seen through careful reading. Harry frequently introduces an unlikable character in a book, becomes interested in that character, and then places him or her in another book that helps explain who the character really is. This occurs in his romances as well as in his coming-of-age books.

Willis was first introduced as a minor character in *The Dollar Man,* written in 1974. In 1978, Harry wrote *The War on Villa Street,* an entire book about Willis. Marcus Rosenbloom, the protagonist of *The Dollar Man* and *I Love You, Stupid!* is recalled by Willis in *The Girl of His Dreams.* "What did that kid Rosenbloom say about you, years ago? That Willis Pierce was the meanest kid in Columbus Junior High?" (126).

Wendy—Marcus's friend and eventual sexual partner in *I Love You, Stupid!*—also appeared *The Dollar Man.* In *The Dollar Man* she is the weird daughter of his mother's best friend, Grace. She wears octagonal granny glasses, a moldy leopard-skin jacket, and a leather thong around her neck with "a dried-up piece of root that looked like a shrunken human figure" (87).

Marcus is surprised when he meets Wendy again in *I Love You, Stupid!* He tells her he is a writer, and in his writer's mode he assesses her:

> *Rugged individualism. . . .*
> > *Modest poverty. . . .*
> > *Enthusiastic type. . . .*
> > *Jumps to conclusions. . . .*
> > *Olympic style. . . .*
> > *An observant type. . . .*
> > *She says nice things too. . . .*
> > *Takes everything too seriously. . . .*
> > *All right. . . .*
> > *Not, you, Miss Leaky Faucet.*
> > *Drip, drip, drip.* (9–11)

Although Harry Mazer's romances have some of the elements of fairy tales, they are far more than the typical formula romances written for and read by many adolescents. They are important books with authentic characters who experience real-life problems. The romances are plot elements which allow the characters to develop and grow.

7. Harry and Norma: Relationship, Romance, and Writing

It is impossible to write about Harry Mazer without discussing his nearly 50-year relationship with Norma Fox Mazer. Their long marriage is based on more than love and family; it is also built on respect and encouragement. In fact, Harry admits that without Norma it is unlikely that he would be writing today. Not only did Norma encourage Harry to give up the jobs that supported the family in order to become a writer but she also supported him emotionally (and, at times, financially) during the long, arduous process of becoming a writer.

Mazer has never found writing easy. Becoming a writer began when he was a teenager and posed as a writer carrying notebooks and pens. When he was 38, with the prodding of Norma, he began to write full time. However, it was not until 1972 that Mazer published his first book, *Guy Lenny,* and not until 1974 that he published his first commercially successful book, *Snow Bound.* In the years before that, he and Norma worked part time at other jobs and practiced the art of writing by publishing nonfiction articles and a story each week for the pulp confession magazines. They were making a living at writing—at one time, nearly $30,000 a year between them—but they were not really fulfilled.

Relationship

You can't be around Harry and Norma Mazer for long without knowing how important they are to each other. The strength of their relationship and the strength of Norma herself help explain, in part, the presence of such strong female characters in all of Mazer's novels. In fact, Harry says it is because of her that he developed his first strong female protagonist, Cindy in *Snow Bound*. In the first draft, Cindy's only response to being stranded in a snowbound car on a deserted plateau was to cry. Norma, who always is the first reader of Harry's drafts, did not worry about hurting his feelings. She simply told him that Cindy didn't work as a character in an adventure story; she needed to be as strong as Tony—she needed to defeat the environment with Tony. Of course, Norma was right.

However, Norma is not always right. She tells a very funny tale she calls the "not me before you, Honey" story. Before the publication of their first novels, Norma told Harry that she would never publish first. She says with a sheepish twinkle, "I thought I needed to protect his male ego." The answer to the question "Whose novel was really published first?" depends on whom you ask. Norma says that her first novel (*I, Trissy*) and Harry's first novel (*Guy Lenny*) were published on the same day. Harry, on the other hand, points out that Norma's novel was accepted before his.

Mazer also maintains that Norma is more commercially successful than he is. He says that she writes faster and produces more and that she is much better with words than he is. Norma disagrees. She says that his books *The Last Mission, Snow Bound,* and *When the Phone Rang* were particularly successful. She admits that she also has had some very well-received books but is hesitant to say whether she or Mazer is the more successful.

The Romance

Harry Mazer met Norma Fox when she was only 15 and he was 21. He remembers the event vividly and uses it, or aspects of it, in several of his novels. He came out from under a car on which he was working and saw Norma for the first time. (At one point Hilary, a character in the Mazers' novel *Heartbeat,* comes out from under a car and sees Tod.) Even at 15 Norma was beautiful.

Mazer knew right away that he was interested in her. He also knew that she was too young. So, other than driving her an hour to her home that day while they talked about books, Harry did not pursue Norma and did not see her for 2 years.

Harry and Norma met again 2 years later—this time, during the 1948 presidential campaign, at a political rally she was attending with her sister. Not only were he and Norma both interested in books, but they also had the same political beliefs. The rally was for the third-party candidate Henry Wallace. Wallace lost the election to Harry Truman, but Harry Mazer won Norma's heart.

Norma and Harry Mazer were drawn together by their common interest in books and things literary. They were both idealists who believed in the power of the working class and in socialism. Norma came from a more literary background than Harry, but he had always loved books, and, indeed, he had lived his life through books. Norma remembers how enlightened he seemed. Now she realizes that his sophistication came not from personal experience but from what he had read in books. He could talk about any topic, and Norma was very impressed by his intelligence.

Although Norma Fox entered college in Ohio, she remained in school for only a little more than a semester. She returned to New York to marry Harry Mazer. Norma was an 18-year-old college freshman, and Harry was 23. Harry admits that Norma was much too young for marriage, but he was ready to get married and didn't want to wait. The first few months of their marriage were spent in New York City, but Norma could not stand the noise and the dirt, and so they moved to Schenectady. During the early years of their married life, Harry had many jobs as a laborer, and Norma had babies, working part time as a cashier or as a salesclerk. Harry was working not only to support his growing family but also to support his political beliefs. It was not until Norma was pregnant with their fourth child and Mazer was frustrated with the menial nature of his jobs—having lost a teaching job and been denied another one because of his political beliefs—that they began writing.

The Writers

One of the things that make Norma and Harry Mazer unique as writers and as a couple is that they write both alone and together. They are not the only team of married writers in the young adult market. Vera and Bill Cleaver wrote together for many years. Other teams also exist in the field of young adult books. The brothers James Lincoln Collier and Christopher Collier are well known for their historical fiction, for example, and professors Lee Irwin and Ann Hadley write under the combined name Hadley Irwin.

However, Harry Mazer and Norma Fox Mazer were for many years a married couple who individually wrote successful young adult novels. Harry talks about their marriage as being a literary marriage, initially based on their common interest in reading and later on their common interest in writing. According to Mazer, it is "first a marriage in fact and then a marriage in fancy" (ALAN Workshop).

Harry and Norma are very different in terms of their approach to writing. Mazer suggests that she is a Type A personality and writer, "calm and reassuring and . . . reasonable and sensitive" (Illinois Librarians). On the other hand, Mazer describes himself as a Type Z personality and writer. When they first began to write, long before they wrote together, Norma spoke to Harry "the way Type A's talk to Type Z's. . . . She said to me, 'You want to write. We want to write. All we have to do is start writing regularly'" (Illinois Librarians).

When Harry protested, saying that he wouldn't have a job if he was a writer, Norma told him to "stop sniveling." She suggested that they write for 15 minutes a day. According to Harry, it was Norma who cracked the whip, and it was Norma who convinced Harry that he could be a writer. "I used to write on the back of order sheets that I'd bring home—we didn't have much money— for economy. Norma would read what I wrote. She never winced. She always kept her face straight" (Illinois Librarians).

Norma does not deny her role in helping Harry become a writer, but she now admits how scared she was for him to leave his paying jobs. For many years she calmed herself by realizing that one or both of them could always go off to work—"do real work," she says, chuckling. She also gives Mazer far more credit than he gives himself for becoming a successful writer. She agrees that they are very different personalities and work very differently. She is "inner driven." She gets up in the morning and begins writing immediately. If she doesn't, she is very restless and unhappy. Harry, on the other hand, is more likely to do other things first. In fact, he talks about his need to write the book in his head before he "puts it on paper" (or, now, enters it into his word processor). However, Norma says that Harry has a "freer personality." She says that he is "more adventurous and willing to break out than I am—in a lot of ways, in doing things and in writing as well." She says that she talks about breaking out—would like to be more adventurous—but when she sits down to write, she is always doing what she always does. Then she admits, however: "I like what I do. I enjoy it. I love it. I love writing about relationships, but I still would like to do something else, but I find it very difficult. I think, in that sense, Harry has more range than I do."[1]

Although Norma continuously encouraged Harry to write, it was clear from the very beginning that she needed to do more than that; she needed to force him to keep writing. He does not disagree with this but believes he would continue to write if she were not there. It is clear that they both agree with Harry's contention that it is difficult for one writer to live with another writer:

> Of course, two writers living together isn't always easy. Writers argue a lot. They're sensitive. They need a lot of praise. They need to be petted. They need to be told what they've written is good. They're full of doubts and never sure that what they've done is good enough, and when one is a Type A and the other is a Type Z, it can be awfully hard.
>
> Type A's get up early in the morning, and they go to their desks and get right to work. And they don't leave their desks till the work is done. Type Z's hate to get up, and they only go to their desks because Type A is there. Then they have to work on

their fingernails and they jump a lot and they have to let the cat out (or in). Type A's always have things to say and write, and they write quickly and they write easily. They always know where their story is going and how it's going to end. Type Z's love to write first lines and then they get stuck. They scratch out, they bite their nails, they panic, and they waste a lot of paper. Type Z's need large wastebaskets. Type Z's are always going to write the great American novel. Then they read what they've written and bang their head against the wall. And they snivel a lot. Type Z's want everything—fame, fortune, millions of readers, good reviews—and they want it all right now. (Illinois Librarians)

Harry maintains that Norma is more helpful to his writing than he is to her writing. She disagrees: "Well, I don't think that's true. I think we really help each other a lot. I know that when I'm working I'm just a mess of anxieties. I am worried and have insecurities about 'Am I doing this right?' I know he thinks the same things. . . . It is very nice to know that someone you can trust will read it for you" (Norma Fox Mazer, interview with author).

In the end, both Mazers recognize how important they are to each other—each of them giving the other credit for his or her impact on the novels, even the ones they write alone. It is a joy simply listening to the two of them talk as they play with new ideas, share thoughts about their work, and examine the processes they use. Their harmonious bantering back and forth—completing one another's thoughts and working through to solutions—has helped each of them in all stages of their writing.

Norma says: "Harry and I have been each other's first and most trusted readers for over twenty years. Not a book, article, or story that either of us has written has ever gone into the world without the other's blessing."[2] But for Norma the process of sharing her work with her most important reader is as difficult as it is for Harry:

When I finished the first draft of *Downtown,* I gave it, as usual, to Harry to read. . . . For several hours Harry read without comment. His silence alarmed and irritated me and I broke into his reading to ask him how it was going.
"Okay."

Okay? "That's all you can say?"
After a moment—"It's a good first draft."
... I was outraged by his stingy estimate and accused him of
being insensitive to my needs as a writer.[3]

Despite her anger at Harry, Norma recognizes the importance of
his criticism. She says that he helps her to be more adventurous,
while she helps him to strengthen the relationships among characters in his books. Norma depends a great deal on Harry's literary opinions. "I really trust his judgment," she says with emphasis, "Although sometimes he tries to cut too much" (Norma Fox
Mazer, interview with author). Harry also trusts Norma's reac-
tions but complains that she always wants him to expand his
work too much.

The Team

In 1977, the Mazers wrote their first novel together: *The Solid
Gold Kid.* Shortly after its completion, they agreed they would
never do another book together. It was more than 10 years before
they published *Heartbeat,* their second joint work, in 1989. Then,
in only 3 years, they published *Bright Days, Stupid Nights.* They
are currently in the planning stages of a fourth joint novel.

I had a conversation with Norma about how two such different
personalities could possibly write as a team. According to her:
"It's a real push-pull. We really fight sometimes because we do
write differently and we do have a different take [on things]. At
its best, we are adding to each other. We are both giving our
strengths" (Norma Fox Mazer, interview with author).

"And at its worst?" I ask her. She hesitates for some time,
laughs, stumbles over her words, and laughs again, saying, "At its
worst, we're really close to divorce." She admits that they frequently joke about writing together. She recalls telling me and
other people shortly after *The Solid Gold Kid* came out, "I'll
never write with that man again!" But she can't remember
exactly why they found it so difficult to work together on that
particular book.

Harry comes up with most of the ideas, but she has a more complete sense of what the finished manuscript will look like. Harry comes up with "the stuff," and Norma is busy linking his pieces together. "That's my strength," she says, "I want things to link together. Well, he does too, but I can do that better than he does" (Norma Fox Mazer, interview with author).

The collaboration for each of their three joint novels has been slightly different, partly because of different technology, partly because of particular circumstances, and partly because of conscious changes they made in how they collaborate.

The Solid Gold Kid was originally Harry's story. Harry had written the first draft of the book, but Norma did not like the characters. As she says, "It was in the drawer" (interview with author). They decided to pull it out of the drawer because it had a lot of plot and movement—something they knew they needed for a joint novel. Norma took the draft and started working on the characters. She can't remember whether after this Harry took it back again or they simply worked on it together until it was completed. She does remember, though, that it was written on an old manual typewriter and that, by the time they were done, each page was made up of many pages cut and stapled together. It was double- and triple-spaced so that there was room for the two writers to cross out and make changes.

The Mazers smile at each other as they describe working on revisions of the novel at their camp in Canada while they were building their rustic cabin. As with all of her own novels and most of Harry's, Norma has a clear sense of where it was written and revised. They recall a photograph they have not seen in some time of the two of them sitting at a table at their summer camp working on the manuscript of *The Solid Gold Kid* with carpentry tools in the background. The imagery is great fun, and Norma tells Harry that she wants to find that picture.

Harry did the first draft of all of their joint books. The second and third novels were intended to be joint works from the beginning. Norma says that after Harry drafts, she has permission to go in and do anything she wants to it. Today they write and revise their manuscripts, individually and jointly, on a computer:

We edit on the computer. I know some people are printing out. . . . What I usually do is either work in capital letters or underline it, or something. I'll just make suggestions. . . . If I think he's overwritten, I'll put an "X" in front of the phrase or the word or something like that. But I wouldn't [wipe it out]. Or, if I wanted to do that I would create another file so that I wouldn't touch the original. I'm very antsy about anybody touching my work. I mean, I listen to Harry, although it's very hard for me still. I hate it when he criticizes my writing. I recognize that probably 99 percent of the time it's justified. (Norma Fox Mazer, interview with author)

Harry breaks in and explains how they have begun working jointly at the computer. He says that while Norma is sitting at the keyboard and he's sitting next to her and they have a problem, he'll "murmur something—sort of a half formed idea, and she'll take it and develop it a little bit more. Then I find it's wonderful . . . because it's almost like a duet" (interview with author).

When they wrote *Heartbeat,* their second joint novel, they talked the whole book out first. Then Harry wrote the first draft, after which Norma took it and tore it to pieces and put it back together again. That's when the conflicts started. When it was his turn with the manuscript, Norma told him, "Don't you dare touch a word" (ALAN Workshop). I asked Norma if it had really happened this way. "It probably did," she said, laughing, "it sounds like something I would say" (Norma Fox Mazer, interview with author).

Then they worked on the manuscript together—several times. They sat side by side at the computer, fighting over lines. This caused a lot of tension, because their writing styles are so different. According to Harry, "I want to condense everything while Norma wants to expand every idea" (ALAN Workshop). Norma agrees with Harry on this point; she says that it's one of the ways she helps him. She remembers that when he wrote *I Love You, Stupid!* they were at their camp in Canada. She was reading and saying, "Tell me more; it's not enough." Harry would start talking, and Norma would write down what he was saying, thus helping him to think through what he wanted to write.

As they wrote and revised *Heartbeat,* they had "constant dis-
agreements, long silences, heavy sighs, [and] deep breathing,"
recalls Harry:

> Norma wanted Tod and Amos to do more than just talk. She gave
> Amos a crate of honeydews to unpack. I objected. "Honeydews
> don't come in crates," I said. "They come in boxes."
>
> "Fine," she said. Norma deletes crate and gives Amos a box
> of honeydews to uncrate. Harry still not satisfied. He wants Tod
> helping Amos. "Fine," Norma says again. "Tod is helping Amos
> unpack a box of honeydews." Harry still not satisfied. "They're
> not unpacking," he says. "They're stacking honeydews on the
> stand."
>
> Norma starts punching the keys. Hyperventilating. "Fine,"
> she yells once more. "They're unpacking a box not a crate of
> honeydews, which they are stacking not putting on the stand."
> (ALAN Workshop)

Norma remembers another of their arguments, about which
she feels she was vindicated. In one of the final scenes in the
book, Tod and Hilary are visiting Amos in the hospital. There is a
very sentimental scene when they all join hands. Norma says they
fought over that scene. "I didn't want it, he did. Wouldn't you
know it," she says, "one of the reviewers picked out that scene"
(Norma Fox Mazer, interview with author). The reviewer said
that *Heartbeat* was a good book, but that moment was flawed.

Norma and Harry negotiate their way through their arguments. They each listen to see if the other person has a valid point
and if their personal ideas should not be held onto so strongly.
When this occurs, Norma says, "you give a little." Sometimes
Norma finds herself thinking: "Maybe he's right. Maybe this is
excessive. Maybe there are too many words" (interview with
author).

The Solid Gold Kid

The Solid Gold Kid, the Mazers' first joint novel, provides a good
example of how Harry has helped Norma break out from her

usual work and become more adventurous. Likewise, a close reading of the book demonstrates how Norma has helped Harry improve his characters and their relationships. This suspense novel was drafted by Harry, who created the strong plot. But because Norma did not like the characters, Harry abandoned it. Her first revision of his draft was done to strengthen the characters and their relationships.

The novel is both a story about relationships and a tale of suspense. Derek has almost no contact with his divorced parents and few friends at his boarding school, and he desperately wants to meet a pretty blond girl whom he sees on his way to the bus stop one rainy Saturday afternoon. His desire to meet her inadvertently puts both of them and several other young people into the midst of a kidnapping plot to abduct Derek, the son of one of the wealthiest men in the country. Reviews, although mixed, have found the story to be fast-paced and exciting (Harry's contribution to the joint work) and the characters to be "developed with empathy and understanding" (Norma's contribution to the work).[4]

Heartbeat

The Mazers' second joint novel was published more than a decade after their first. *Heartbeat* is about an unusual love triangle among three young people. Tod is handsome but shy and has never had a girlfriend. His more gregarious friend, Amos—who once saved Tod's life following a swimming accident—is short, cute, and funny. Amos falls for Hilary and asks Tod to return his lifesaving favor as he has promised. Tod reluctantly agrees to talk to Hilary for Amos. And he really does try. Not unpredictably, however, Tod and Hilary fall in love. Tod doesn't know how to tell Amos of his and Hilary's involvement.

Although the plot is a typical love triangle, borrowed from *Cyrano de Bergerac* or John Alden in *The Courtship of Miles Standish,* it expands beyond the formula when Amos is hospitalized with a viral infection that has permanently weakened his heart. As the friends learn that Amos may not survive, Tod tells Hilary of his promise and his deception. Hilary decides to pretend that she is in love with Amos while he is in the hospital. Tod feels both guilt and jealousy. Not surprisingly, Hilary does come to love Amos. After his death, it is clear to both Tod and Hilary that they can't go back to the way they had been before.

This is a wonderful teenage romance. Many reviewers discuss the "strong, nonsterotypical characterization."[5] Hilary, for example, is not particularly beautiful, and she hides her best feature, her hair, under a cap as she works as a mechanic. Tod is handsome; however, he is also shy and has a difficult life with his destructive Vietnam vet father. Before Hilary, he has never had a girlfriend. Amos is fun and gregarious and has always had girlfriends, but he asks his friend Tod to fix him up with Hilary. One can see Norma Mazer's deft touch in the character development and intertwining relationships in the novel. Trish Ebbatson in a *School Library Journal* review suggests that the strength of the story "lies in the characters' relationships with each other, their feelings of obligation and commitment, and an understanding of when the needs of the others take priority."[6]

Harry Mazer's crafting of plot can also be seen in the novel. As Zena Sutherland suggests in a review in the *Bulletin of the Center for Children's Books*, "It's a moving story, psychologically intricate and convincing, that explores the conflict between romantic love and loyalty to a friend in a way that is broader than the immediate situation of the story."[7] Other reviewers call it "fast-paced"[8] with a "strong narrative sense [that] keeps the reader engaged."[9]

Heartbeat is a joint novel that allows us to see the team of Harry and Norma Fox Mazer at its best. The characters are well drawn and realistic, avoiding the stereotypes of typical teenage romances. Each of the multidimensional characters seems to be the opposite of what his or her appearance suggests.

The novel is told from Tod's point of view. Throughout, his voice is clearly heard. This allows us to feel his frustration, fear, awkwardness, caring, and guilt. We come to really care about what happens to him. If Amos, the victim of the strange disease, had told the story, it could have become maudlin. Since it is told in Tod's voice, it is empathetic and moving without being melodramatic. It is Harry Mazer's ability to develop a clear voice—a voice that is authentic—that makes Tod such a strong character.

Several chapters throughout the novel, printed in italics, are told from Hilary's point of view. Hilary's chapters are written in the first person, whereas those told from Tod's point of view are written in the third person. Harry recalls that he tried this technique in *Snow Bound*—having Tony tell the story in first person and Cindy in third. In this way, he believed their voices would be clearly distinguished. However, Ron Buehl, his editor, did not think it worked, finding it too confusing for young readers. So Harry revised *Snow Bound,* writing it entirely in the third person.

One thing that both Harry and Norma, alone and together, have continued to experiment with is changing viewpoints. Even as they are working on a novel, they change the viewpoint from first to third person, thereby adding another layer to the character. Harry admits that he has even changed a character's gender to see how the different point of view will affect dialogue, attitudes, and emotions. He can't remember doing this in any of his novels, although he thinks he might in a forthcoming work; but he has done this "sex change" in the work he and Norma did for confession magazines—their "pulp work," as Harry calls it. Norma suggests that if you think about how your character would change by altering the gender, even if you do not do so in the novel, you add depth. Harry agrees. Perhaps this is why Harry's characters are multidimensional—why both his male and his female characters are so realistic, sympathetic, and authentic.

The use of shifting person does work in *Heartbeat,* even if it didn't work in *Snow Bound.* Perhaps it works because so few chapters (7 out of 41) are from Hilary's point of view, and only Tod's world is described in detail. The use of third person is necessary for us to learn more about Tod than he can tell us, and it allows us to hear an older and wiser Tod as he reflects on what he has learned about friendship, family, and love. We don't need to learn as much about Hilary. It is sufficient to see her from Tod's point of view. However, her 7 chapters and periodic sentences or brief paragraphs add interest and depth to the novel.

Tod's difficult relationship with his father—another trademark of Harry Mazer's novels—adds to the interesting fabric of the work. Tod's father has never fully recovered from his wife's death. Tod resents his father's habit of picking up stakes and moving. He also dislikes they way his father treats women and how he disregards him. However, like young Harry Mazer, Tod loves his father and feels torn and guilty about their strained relationship.

This relationship provides one of the interesting subplots of the novel and adds another dimension to Tod's character. Another subplot is Tod's longtime friendship with Amos, a friendship that becomes strained when he falls in love with Hilary as he attempts but fails to tell her about Amos. This plot line is further complicated when Amos develops a serious, life-threatening disease that forces a permanent wedge between Tod and Hilary.

Another strength of this romantic novel—one that is characteristic of all of Harry Mazer's romances—is that the sexual relationship between Tod and Hilary is neither avoided nor exploited. At times, such as in the woods following a particularly difficult visit with Amos in the hospital, their physical needs for each other are communicated. Yet the novel does not go into detail about their sexual relationship. As in all of Harry Mazer's romances, the characters come to understand that there is far more to life than sex and even romantic love. As Tod realizes this, he releases Hilary to help Amos while he is dying. To the end, however, Tod remains an authentic adolescent. His feelings are conflicted. He loves Hilary and cares deeply about Amos. He feels guilt about their deception and yet is jealous about Hilary's relationship with Amos. At the same time, he knows that he must attempt to save Amos's life, just as Amos had saved his. The moment at the end of the novel in which Amos draws Tod's and Hilary's hands together—a scene Norma fought to remove because she thought it seemed contrived—lets us know that Amos has not been deceived. He recognizes Tod's love for Hilary, and he accepts and understands Tod's tremendous act of friendship.

Again, like all of Harry Mazer's romances, the novel does not end with the two protagonists living "happily ever after." It is clear that they have both gained maturity, but they have lost each other. Their relationship can never be as it was. Tod's relationship with his father has improved somewhat, and Tod is beginning to accept his father's girlfriend, Loretta. He is going off to England to visit his grandmother (his mother's mother). Tod and Hilary say good-bye at her house. She tells him to write. The final line of the books is what Tod writes on a postcard to Hilary, "*Someday . . .*"

Bright Days, Stupid Nights

Bright Days, Stupid Nights is the most recent novel written jointly by Harry and Norma Mazer. It, too, is an interesting romance that has a complicated, twisted plot; multidimensional, nonstereotypical actors; and important ethical challenges for the characters. It is told from the perspective of the two major characters: the 14-year-old, precocious Vicki Barfield and the independent dreamer, Chris Georgiade. Joining them in the novel are two other summer interns on a Pulitzer Prize–winning newspaper: talkative Elizabeth and poised Faith. Both are beautiful, rich, and sophisticated. Vicki, on the other hand, had to lie about her age to get the internship. And Chris had to accept the internship against his father's wishes.

This novel is told in two equal voices. Both Vicki and Chris tell their stories from the third-person point of view. Reviewer Cindy Darling Codell suggests that the alternating viewpoints "keep this story from having the flow and urgency of the Mazers' *The Solid Gold Kid.*"[10] Although third person may eliminate some of our feeling of urgency, it is a device that allows us to get to know the characters not only from their own perspectives but also from the perspectives of others. Because of the ethical dilemma that is central to the plot of this novel, this distance from each character's point of view is essential. We get to know Vicki and Chris very well; we know about their families, their thoughts, their fears, and their dreams.

Vicki, who looks older than her 14 years, is the daughter of a single mother who has high expectations for her. She is encouraged to take the internship even though it means lying about her age. Although she is fearful, her mother convinces her that she must go. Her awkwardness and immaturity are obvious when she first arrives at the rooming house in Scottsville, Pennsylvania, and meets Mrs. Roos, the landlady, and Faith and Elizabeth. She keeps hearing her mother's voice: *"Vicki sweetie, no negative thinking. . . . You're going to be great!"*

Chris is also an interesting, well-developed character. He is much like Harry Mazer was as an adolescent and is an interesting parallel to Marcus in *I Love You, Stupid!* Chris's family is large and has a Greek heritage. His father, like Mazer's own, is a laborer. Chris, however, wants to be a writer and go to college. His father disapproves and thinks he should find a "real job." Chris feels like a duck out of water in his home. Both his father and his brother are good at working on engines, but he's all thumbs. His father never stops talking about his immigrant heritage. Chris is not ashamed of his family; he's just different from them. He wins the internship after submitting an essay about his family's peculiar habits, parts of which appear in the first chapter of the novel. When Chris's father says that he must take the summer job at Kirkland and not accept the internship, Chris runs away and sends his acceptance without his father's permission.

Elizabeth and Faith, the other two interns, are mysterious by intention. We learn about Elizabeth's family only from what she says about them, and we learn almost nothing about Faith's family until Vicki discovers stories about Faith's father in the newspaper's "morgue." Whether or not to write an article about Faith and her family's questionable past—full of intrigue, wealth, and controversy—is one of the ethical dilemmas of the novel. Does the public have a right to know? Do innocent people deserve protection from the media? Vicki and Faith argue about whether the story should be written:

> "Oh, yes. You are good, Faith. That's what is so intriguing. I mean . . . I come from a poor family and I *have* to be good. But you are good anyway. You could have just leaned back on your laurels, your money, or whatever."
>
> Faith was silent. She looked at Vicki in a way she never had before. "This has been a good summer for me so far. I've felt safe. I've met some wonderful people, it's been good. I want to leave it at that. I want you to put what you read about my family out of your mind."
>
> "I can't, Vicki said. "A famous person being a humble intern is so unusual. That's the angle for my story, that's you, Faith, no stuck up airs." . . .
>
> "Vicki, try to hear me. I'm not famous. It's my father, not me!"[11]

Through this incident we learn more about all of the characters. Their argument nearly turns into a tragedy when the interns side with Faith and decide to teach Vicki a lesson by locking her in an old truck. She escapes, kicking her foot through a window, fearing that she will suffocate and die. Sounds she hears in the darkness make her remember incidents from her past—incidents that make us better understand Vicki and her need to succeed and be recognized:

> A high pitched drone like a dentist's drill reached her ears. Cicadas. In fifth grade she'd done an oral report on cicadas. Mr. Hegaman, a teacher she loved and wanted to impress, had let her do the whole report pronouncing it Sigh-kah-da. . . . "Cicadas are insects that live on trees and shrubs. Cicadas produce their sharp clicking sound by vibrating a membrane beneath their abdomen. . . ."
>
> Then, when she was through he'd said, "The correct pronunciation is si-KA-da, Vicki. You should have looked it up." She'd been so stunned she burst into tears in front of everyone. (151–52)

Reviewer Stephanie Zvirin suggests that the plot is "deliberate, rather slow," and it "drags," but that "the characters are, for the most part, distinct."[12] Zena Sutherland has a similar concern, calling the novel "a padded situation-exploration."[13] It is true that this novel does not have the suspense and excitement of *The Solid Gold Kid*. However, the characters are far better developed. This novel is a character study, more typical of most of the Mazers' individual novels, rather than a novel that focuses on plot and action. It is appropriate reading for more mature adolescents who are interested in finding out why people behave as they do.

Vicki runs away after returning to the boardinghouse to pack her things. When the other interns become concerned and go back to the truck, they discover Vicki is gone. Chris realizes with horror what they have done to her. Vicki has no idea where she will go, but she boards a bus headed north, the first bus leaving Scottsville. When the bus drops her off in Oneonta, she can't decide if she will go home and admit defeat or return to Scottsville. Along the way, she has thought of what the others have said about her. They called her "a gossip journalist" and said that she was an "opportunist." Elizabeth had defined that for her, saying it was someone who "takes advantage of any situation without regard to anybody else" (157). She wonders if she is wrong, if the only thing she wanted to do is win. Would she have to admit she was wrong to everyone? Vicki is alone, afraid, believing that everyone hates her when a car pulls up and she hears a man say, "I told you it was a girl." She runs. With nowhere to go and no one to turn to, she decides to call Chris. Through this incident we also learn more about Chris and his family. Despite the long drive, Chris goes to pick up Vicki. They go to a diner and argue about whether she should return to Scottsville. Vicki says that everyone hates her. Chris replies: "'Vicki, it's not hate. You know how Faith feels. And Elizabeth wants to protect Faith. And I think that journalism should be put to better use, especially by somebody as talented as you. . . . The crux, Vicki, is that we hate what you want to do, not you'" (172).

Underlying the entire novel is a romance—actually, several romances. Vicki is in love with Chris, although it takes him the entire novel to realize it. Chris is in love with Elizabeth but is constantly confronted with her talk about her boyfriend, Ira. Chris turns himself into Crash, a romantic character in the novel he is attempting to write: *"Thumbs in his belt loops, radiating an easy calm. Crash moved across the parking lot. Eyes darted toward him, then away. Shoulders seemed to expand visibly. Our territory, outlanders"* (57). Only after Chris and Vicki go to the county fair together in search of a good article and she admits to him that she is only 14 does he begin to understand that when she is acting foolish, she is acting her age and trying to impress him: "Later, the Big Light of Understanding flashed on in his brain. It had taken him all these weeks to understand that Vicki wanted something from him: the same something he wanted from Elizabeth" (105). Throughout the novel Chris is becoming less and less satisfied with working at the newspaper. He realizes that much of the work is boring and takes no talent. The interns run errands and write obituaries and cut lines for pictures; they do little real reporting. He thinks of himself as fictionalizing everything but has no idea where he is going with his novel. Chris, like all of the interns, is trying to find himself apart from his family, and he is frustrated by the process.

Like all of Harry Mazer's romances and those he has written with Norma Fox Mazer, this novel does not end with the girl in the arms of the boy, who has finally realized that he does love her. Instead, the characters have found friendship. They have discovered each other's limitations and strengths and have decided to remain friends. The Mazers use the same technique at the end of this novel as at the end of their other two joint novels: The characters write letters to each other. These letter sum up the novel— sometimes perhaps a bit too neatly—and let readers decide what will occur next.

Even when writing individually, Harry Mazer and Norma Fox Mazer are a team. They may write alone, but they talk about what they are going to write, read what the other has written, help each other limit or expand what has been written, criticize each other's work, and celebrate each other's successes. They are proud of their work alone and their work together. Both realize that they are fine writers individually but that their individual strengths help make each other's work better. As Harry Mazer says, he thinks of their best writing together as a "duet." It is a duet with fine harmony, both in their marriage and in their work. Harry Mazer, author and man, is complex, thoughtful, caring, honest, and an authentic human being. His books, both alone and with Norma, reflect his life and his personality.

8. Harry Mazer:
A Writer for
Generations of Teenagers

Why Are Harry Mazer's Books Important?

Harry Mazer's books are popular with adolescents and critically acclaimed by adults. Teenagers have chosen many of his books to include on the "Young Adult Choice" and the "Children's Choice" lists, both prepared by the International Reading Association (IRA) and the Children's Book Council (CBC), and on the "Iowa Teen Award" list. For each of these lists, adolescents select the books they consider the "best" of the year. *The Solid Gold Kid, Hey, Kid! Does She Love Me? When the Phone Rang, The Girl of His Dreams,* and *Heartbeat* all have appeared on these teen-chosen lists. Teachers, librarians, and literary critics also consider many of Mazer's books as among the best published for young readers. The American Library Association (ALA) has included seven of his books on the "Best Books for Young Adults" list in the year they published: *The Solid Gold Kid, The War on Villa Street, The Last Mission, I Love You, Stupid! When the Phone Rang, The Girl of His Dreams,* and *Who Is Eddie Leonard?* In addition, *The Last Mission* was selected by ALA as a best book for young adults for the years from 1970 through 1983. Starred reviews in *Booklist, School Library Journal,* and *Kirkus Reviews*—three important literary review journals—have been awarded to *The Dollar Man, The War on Villa Street, I Love You,*

Stupid! Hey, Kid! Does She Love Me? When the Phone Rang, and *The Girl of His Dreams.* The New York Public Library has placed *The Last Mission, Hey, Kid! Does She Love Me? The Girl of His Dreams,* and *Heartbeat* on its short recommended list, "Books for the Teen Age." The *New York Times* called *The Last Mission* a best book for the year 1979 and *The Island Keeper,* which was also a Junior Literary Guild selection, a "new and noteworthy paperback" in 1981.

Mazer's books have also been recognized outside the United States. *Snow Bound* has been translated into French, German, and Finnish. *The Last Mission* will soon be published in German. *When the Phone Rang* received the West Australian Young Readers' Book Award. In addition, *Snow Bound* was produced as a television movie in both the United States and Germany.

These awards and recognitions by both adolescents and adults prove that Mazer's books are well received. But they are important for another reason, as well. They are widely read by adolescent readers, who find them believable and interesting, and most of his books are still in print. Their continuing popularity is remarkable. Many of the books Mazer wrote and published in the 1970s and 1980s are now being read by the teenage children of parents who read them as teenagers. What better way to make a connection between the generations than to have them share in common relationships with characters in books they have come to love? Mazer's characters are as believable to teenagers today as they were to their parents more than 20 years ago.

Harry Mazer's books are also important because they are representative of an important genre in American literature. According to David Peck in *Novels of Initiation,* much of American literature focuses on adolescence. And because it focuses on adolescence, much of American literature deals with the themes of coming of age, loss of innocence, and rebellion. He claims that American literature is relatively young literature and that, like America's predominantly adolescent culture, the literature has been "essentially an adolescent literature—which is one of the reasons many of the classics of American literature can be taught in high school literature, and are."[1] Peck cites the following authors in his argument: J. D. Salinger, Mark Twain, Sylvia Plath, F. Scott Fitzgerald, Stephen Crane, Harper Lee, Carson McCullers, and John Steinbeck. Therefore, Peck suggests, young adult literature—literature written specifically for an adolescent audience—has a very comfortable niche in American literature.

Although all young adult literature could be classified as coming-of-age literature, there is a specific genre that focuses on the growth of the adolescent from childhood to adulthood—usually on the psychological and sexual growth. This is the literature whose theme is adolescence, the period of transition from the usually carefree life of childhood to the increased responsibility of adulthood. During this phase, young adults experience isolation, socialization, confusion, and rebellion. They desire to return to dependence on the family and at the same time to forge ahead into the unknown. Teenagers seek the support of a peer group and at the same moment are fiercely individualistic and independent. These are the topics that occupy the plots of Mazer's coming-of-age books. Because Mazer has written 15 books that explore this genre, he is one of the premier authors of adolescent literature.

In addition, Mazer's books are important because most of them address the coming of age of males. The protagonists in his books are not the well-to-do young men of earlier coming-of-age literature (*A Separate Peace, Catcher in the Rye);* they are the children of blue-collar workers who struggle to get through *public* high schools, who work because they have to, who see college as an unlikely dream. His protagonists are real adolescents, and his books are important in that they can be read and enjoyed by adolescents who are nonreaders because they do not see themselves on the pages of books assigned by teachers. In fact, one of Mazer's novels, *Heartbeat,* written with Norma Fox Mazer, has been cited as one of the best books for reluctant young adult readers. Mazer says of his writing:

> When I started writing I had no idea I would find myself writing for young readers. My agent suggested I do something in this area, and I discovered that I liked writing about this time of life. Adolescence for me was so intense, so filled with joy, pain,

expectations, hope, despair, energy, that though those years are
far behind me they remain real to me, and have a vividness and
clarity that events much closer to me in time do not have. I discovered a 13-year-old voice inside me.[2]

When asked why his books are important and why someone
would want to write or read a book about him, Mazer modestly
chuckles and responds, "Well, I've been around for a long time."
After a few minutes of reflection, he answers more thoughtfully:

Why are my books important? They're important because
they're honest, and they are written with real guilt. . . . There is
integrity in the work so it's effective, not hokey. I have a great
belief in workmanship, good work, solid work, work that is well
founded, has a structure with a foundation, a cellar and walls
and a roof—it stands. (interview with author)

Harry Mazer's books are important because they deal honestly
with authentic adolescent characters who are learning how to
become men and women. All young adult literature could be
called coming-of-age literature because it focuses on adolescent
protagonists. A distinguishing feature of the young adult novel,
according to novelist Richard Peck, is that "it needs to end at a
beginning."[3] The 15-year-old has not yet begun to live life; the
best and worst still lie ahead. The events of the young adult novel,
therefore, must prepare the reader and the book's protagonist for
a life yet to be lived. Mazer does this successfully in his books
because, as he says, he deals primarily with the character's "inner
life. Not the trappings of character but their feelings, their
dreams and fantasies, the way they distort reality, their hopes
and disappointments."[4] For this reason, readers come to know
Mazer's characters and can see themselves in their lives.

Mazer is able to capture the authentic voices and inner lives of
adolescents in his novels. His adolescents deal with issues, tell
stories, ask questions. The voices of Mazer's adolescent characters are eternal voices—voices that come from him and his generation as well as voices that span the years to today's adolescents
who read his books. The intergenerational nature of his charac-

ters' voices pleases Mazer because he believes that literature, at its best—real literature—must have authentic voices that speak to more than the world they come out of.

Can an Adult Author Write for a Young Adult Reader?

The British critic John Yandell suggests in his column in *New Statesman and Society* that the preoccupation with the development of the adolescent is one of the problems of the field of young adult literature, and he uses Mazer's *The Girl of His Dreams* as an example of the problem:

> At the center of teenage fiction lies a contradiction: read by and written about teenagers, written and marketed by adults. Looking for a particular kind of (linear) coherence to their own stories, adults tend to conceive of adolescence as a staging-post along the road to adulthood; teenagers, on the other hand, are more interested in being than in becoming. It often seems as if the self-appointed task of the teenage novel is to tell its readers what they must become.[5]

Ironically, it may be because of this that coming-of-age literature is so important. Literature is one means by which the adolescent can explore the passage from childhood to adulthood. Readers who typically do not find themselves on the pages of books can explore their own coming of age through Mazer's books. As Peck writes, "The adolescent in America . . . is often in a kind of social and psychological limbo, someone with limited economic power but no real status, treated as a child by parents and teachers, but with social, sexual, and cultural sophistication that sometimes belies this position. . . . Reading literature about themselves helps teenagers to define their own identity and to develop their own values."[6] The characters in Mazer's books face many of the problems of maturing from childhood to adulthood, and his books allow young adults, particularly males, to examine themselves using the protagonist as a model. According to young adult author Lloyd Alexander, "A [good young adult] book should speak to readers not only where they are . . . but where they will be."[7] Mazer talks about this search for identity as the "most fundamental aspect of adolescence—to know who you are, to know what your place is in the world, to know where you belong" (interview with author). With warmth and wisdom, Mazer's books help adolescents accomplish this search. They speak directly to adolescents, never down to them. At the same time his books provide readers with mature insights into their own lives. According to critic Kenneth Donelson, "Harry Mazer writes about young people caught in the midst of moral crises, often of their own making. . . . Searching for a way out, they discover themselves, or rather they learn that the first step in extricating themselves from their physical and moral dilemmas is self-discovery. Intensely moral as Harry's books are, they present young people thinking and talking and acting believably."[8]

Mazer is not immune to criticism about the problems of adults writing for and about young adults. Sometimes he wonders how a middle-age man with "gray in my chin" can write for the young. He answers his own concerns with a question:

> But how many books are there written by writers under 20, or 25, for that matter? A handful maybe. There's a rightness in the old—I mean, of course, the mature—writing for the young. The young, after all, are young, they're impatient, they've got ants in their pants. I wonder if they can sit still long enough to give form to their own thoughts and feelings. (At that age I couldn't.) Maybe the trappings of dress and manner have changed, but the emotions of the young are not a foreign country. We've all been there. We recognize our ties to the young, even when they don't recognize their ties to us.[9]

However, Mazer ponders the question of whether the monitoring—including the reviewing and selecting—of books for adolescents by so many adults makes it impossible for authors to write "real literature" for kids. He claims that it is possible to write good books for kids—serious books with well-developed characters. However, he puzzles over whether it is possible today to write real literature, literature with an authentic literary voice. He worries about the "presence of guardians all around children's books"—the parents and teachers and librarians who review, in the broadest sense, books for young people. It's very difficult for them to "not get into the bones of the writer and this puts caution into the heart of the writer." But, at the same time, he acknowledges that, at its best, this presence can make books better—"more artful" (interview with author). Norma Fox Mazer suggests that, at least in one case, this presence made one of Harry's books better and, in fact, changed *The Island Keeper* completely. Mazer placed his protagonist Cleo alone on an island in a Canadian lake. This allowed him to avoid the issue of sex by getting rid of the boyfriends. "If she had not been on an island without boys, it might not have been as good a book—it would have taken away from Cleo," suggests Norma (Norma Fox Mazer, interview with author).

Suggesting that Mazer has answered his own question about whether it is possible to write "real literature" for kids by writing novels with authentic voices that span the generations causes him to respond modestly, giving the credit to the kids who read his books. "I think in reading kids are more mature. When kids read you bring out the best in them; they become more mature." According to Mazer, it is through reading that kids come in contact with their inner worlds, the worlds of the soul, the spirit. This is the world he wants to touch, the world he wants to put his readers in touch with. "Reading is a private matter; it's a good friend," he concludes (interview with author). Perhaps it is this inner world, the world of the soul and spirit, captured in Mazer's books that make them real literature: important books for young adults.

Caring and Censorship

Mazer takes seriously his responsibility to write books that give back his readers' "best and purest selves." He says that authors and teachers must "give kids a real literature. A literature that speaks to them, that holds up and mirrors their lives and gives it back to them concentrated and focused in all its diversity" (ALAN Workshop). It is not that Mazer wants to write books that help kids; instead, he sees the help as coming from the people in kids' lives who care about them. In fact, he does not think of literature as useful. "I try not to write useful books," he says. The only use for a story is the story itself:

> In the telling . . . and in the listening, in the reading and losing oneself in the unexpected. The novel puts us into a world we can't alter, a world more interesting, intense, and moving than the real world. A world where nothing useful is expected of us, where things happen that we need only observe, wonder at, and think about.
>
> When we read a novel, when we surrender ourselves to the story, our guard drops, and we abandon our slit-eyed purposefulness. We don't have to pretend, we don't have to put on masks, we don't have to posture and behave usefully. We are released.
>
> There we have it—the true use of a novel—it gives us back our purest selves.[10]

Mazer speaks from experience when he says of literature that it "opens our eyes and our hearts to other lives. It takes us out of our narrowness and isolation. It deals with the spirit and with the heart of things" (Illinois Librarians). Literature, according to Mazer, is all about "shape, order, meaning and hope. Stories hold us. But they also open our eyes and our hearts. They take us out of our narrowness and isolation" (ALAN Workshop). It is because books had this kind of meaning in his life that he takes his art so seriously, that he works so diligently to write books that give young people back their purest selves.

When Mazer talks about his own books, he says that he doesn't like defending them to potential censors—although he does, and he has. According to Mazer, "My books are what they are. A book is a construction. It's the sum of its parts. It's like a house, but it's more complicated than a house. Like a house, you can't start pulling bricks and expect the house to stand." That's what censors do, he says, they "pull bricks" (Illinois Librarians).

Recently Mazer responded to a censorship issue surrounding his book *The Last Mission*. He finds it ironic that censors would pull apart the bricks of this book and focus on a few words when the story is about what happens to a person who experiences a war. The language in the book was toned down to fit the audience; it is not the language that Mazer and his friends really spoke as they flew bombing mission after mission. It is not the language of frustration and fear. Instead, it is a modified language that will allow young readers to experience the horrors of war and still be permitted to read the book.

It is this toned-down language that was recently attacked by censors, a small group of parents of middle-school students, who successfully had the book removed from the library shelves of Carroll Middle School in Southlake, Texas. Mazer agreed to be interviewed about the incident for an article in the *Fort Worth Star-Telegram*. He told the reporter, Yamil Berard, "I could not write this book without the language in the book. The language is like the mortar in the wall of the building."[11] Following the appearance of Berard's article, Mazer wrote in a letter to the reporter: "Words are my business. I think about words all the time and I thought a lot about the language in *The Last Mission*. To begin with I don't divide language into good words and bad words. Words are neither good nor bad. Words are ways to express ideas, concepts, and feelings. They're appropriate or not, they say what you mean or they don't. But more important the words the parents found objectionable are in the book because this is a book about war and these words are the language of war."

As a mature writer, Mazer worries about his art and the effects the world has on his writing. He frequently writes and speaks about censorship and how it influences and changes his books. He says that he likes to think that censors have had no effect on his writing:

> I think that I resist; I do resist; I don't give ground; I write my books exactly the way I've always written them, aware that I'm writing for young people, but also aware that there is a reality out there that I want reflected in my work. But, in saying all

that, I must add that I write today with an awareness and, yes, a caution that wasn't there when I began writing. I've become "inventive" in my use of language, finding other ways of saying what may be challenged.[12]

When Mazer talks of censorship, he is reflective; but when he talks about the accusation made by some censors that his books drive a wedge between parents and their children, he is angry. "Not my books," he says with conviction. "The censors themselves drive the wedge. Each time they ignore their kids' questions and concerns and demand behavior [according] to an arbitrary and unrealistic standard, they drive the wedge even deeper."[13] Mazer writes to the reporter Berard: "I'm glad when parents interest themselves enough in what their children are reading that they, too, read the books. But picking words out of a book is not reading the book, just as picking raisins out of the pot is not eating the pudding."[14]

Are Harry Mazer's Books Pornographic?

Some critics have suggested that Mazer's books dealing with teenagers' dreams about sex are pornographic. But these critics miss the pain and the frustration experienced by the teenagers in the books. They miss the moral endings in which the teenagers learn, even if the critics do not, that real relationships are far more fulfilling than dreams of sex. In an unpublished letter to a Mr. Parker—defending the novel *I Love You, Stupid!*—Mazer wrote,

> Pornography if it means anything is work produced to titillate sexually. In male pornography women are treated as objects to be turned and used and manipulated in any way that the male can imagine. It's unrealistic, it's absurd, it's mean spirited. It has little to say about the real relations of males and females.[15]

In Mazer's books female characters are treated with respect. That does not mean that the male teenage protagonists do not dream of sexual conquests, but it does mean that the females are most often the ones who show the males that sex is only one small part of a relationship. It is the females who prove to the males that it takes more than dreams to succeed, and it is the females who help the males realize their dreams at the same time as they realize their own. Mazer's female characters are strong and authentic. They are not sexually exploited either by the male characters (although they might initially make the attempt) or by the author himself. These are moral books; they are as far from pornography as one can get.

Today and Tomorrow

Harry Mazer, who has just passed his seventieth birthday, has no thought of retiring or slowing down. He enjoys his life too much. He is still learning to be a writer, a better writer. Even beyond 70, he is still searching. When somebody does something that interests him, he still says, "I could do that!" Or he asks himself, "Could I do that?" However, something else comes along with being 70, a feeling he does not like, a feeling that says, "No, you're not going to do that." This feeling of self-doubt, Mazer maintains, is just part of his adolescent mind, the doubting part that says, "You can do this—no you can't." This kind of ambivalence has existed throughout his life. "As my father would have said, it's just plain stupid." "No," says Norma, "What your father would have said was, 'Don't be foolish.'" Or, adds Harry, "What are you talking about?" But with Mazer's continuing belief in himself being tainted with self-doubt there comes a commitment to the future: "'What are you talking about?' That's a good name for a short story."(Harry Mazer and Norma Fox Mazer, interview with author)

Mazer has several projects in the works and at least one "in the drawer." He is currently negotiating a three-book contract for a set he is calling his "dog trilogy." His three working titles are *Dog in the Freezer,* about a boy who attempts to bury his dog in New York City; *My Life as a Dog,* a title he had long before the movie; and *The Dog Ate It,* a novel about a boy who blames everything that happens to him on his dog.

Another project that Mazer has pursued on and off for many years is a novel about the Holocaust. He thinks about this project quite often but has yet to find a way to integrate World War II Europe into his world. Emotionally he understands the Holocaust, but he did not experience it; and Mazer writes from his own life. A few years ago he interviewed a survivor of the Warsaw ghetto—a cigarette seller as a boy who found his way under the wall and survived even after his family had disappeared. He had gone in and out of the ghetto and found food and brought it back. He had had all kinds of incredible experiences. Sometimes he would climb over the wall, putting his coat over the broken glass on top to avoid cutting his hands. "I interviewed him, did a tape, and I haven't done anything with it since," Mazer says with regret (interview with author). But this is not the first project he has put in the drawer. The book that became *The Solid Gold Kid* was drafted and abandoned by him only to be revived some years later. The Holocaust novel may yet be written.

Mazer is also writing a true narrative for younger adolescents, to appear in a book about personal experiences of historic events. Mazer's true narrative will focus on the final days of *his* war—not when *his* war ended, because it will live with him always, but that fearful moment when he believed it was ending:

> It's that terrible moment because there's the fear that you could be killed even though the war is over. You're still fighting. In *All Quiet on the Western Front* this is exactly what happened. . . . In a sense it's what happened to us—killed in the last mission of the war. . . . There is a lot of emotional stuff going on. That's one of the things that struck me. Here it is 50 years, to be exact, after the end of the war in Europe, and it's still going on. (interview with author)

Mazer has several other projects in the works. He is editing an anthology of stories about guns. He has queried young adult authors asking if they have written a story about a gun or would consider writing one. Harry says he has mixed feelings about guns but is neither revolted by them nor enamored of them:

I wouldn't want this book to be a polemic for one or the other view. The gun is out there, it's a reality. It pulls meaning in. It's part of our fantasies, or fears. We believe that guns and freedom are inseparable. It's our ultimate defiance of authority. I wouldn't like to do the obvious, the power, the danger and abuse of the gun. But what about a love story about a gun, or how it caused a relationship to develop.[16]

Harry and Norma Mazer are also busy discussing a joint book they have agreed to write. And he's thinking about an additional short-story anthology. Finally, he's wondering whether to write a true narrative about "my father and me." Maybe, he says, this will be his first adult book. No, Harry Mazer is not retiring, and he is not slowing down. He asks "What's next?" and replies, "Tune in tomorrow" (interview with author).

And so this complex man—this kind man, this modest man who only recently has begun to think of himself as a writer—no longer needs to pose. Today, Mazer is a husband, a father of four grown children, and a very successful and busy author. He speaks of his children with a kind of awe, wondering how they could possibly have become who they are, but knowing all the time that he and Norma and books helped form them. The Mazers' oldest daughter, Anne, who is today the mother of two young children and a very successful author and editor, remembers growing up with the clack of typewriters. She recalls stories being written and talked about. According to Mazer, his kids read. Books, he says, were everywhere, and everybody read. He also recalls that all four of his and Norma's children were good writers, and each had a personal library. Anne has published eight books: three picture books, two edited anthologies of short stories, and three successful novels. Mazer says that she has joined his and Norma's writing circle. "Manuscripts go back and forth, by mail, and fax and computer disk. We read and edit for one another."[17] Susan, the Mazers' third child, has collaborated on her first book—a picture book—with Norma. And, Gina, their youngest daughter, has published poetry. Currently the only nonwriter in the family is son Joe. But, he, too, has followed in his father's footsteps and is a carpenter and teacher.

To date, Harry Mazer has written 14 critically acclaimed novels on his own and 3 more with Norma Fox Mazer. He is busy on a half dozen new projects. When he thinks back to his teenage years, he remembers himself as an overweight, introspective young man who posed as a writer but who didn't write. Although at the time there was a voice within him that denied everything he dreamed of, he now recognizes how important his posing was to his growth as a writer. The voice would ask Harry: "What do you know? What have you written?" He never knew where that disembodied voice came from, but the voice has never entirely left him. Over the years, he has called it different things: the no-sayer, the doubter, the tormenter, the destroyer. But despite that voice's suggesting that he give up his dream of writing—that he had nothing to write which anyone would pay him for—he continued to pose, to see himself as a writer. And today he is a writer who respects his own talent and his own gifts. He says of his writing, "I think I write my life" (interview with author).

Notes and References

1. Harry Mazer: A Country Man in the City

1. Harry Mazer, interview with author, 3 March 1985; hereafter cited in text.
2. "Mazer, Harry," in *Fifth Book of Junior Authors and Illustrators,* ed. Sally H. Holtze (Bronx, N.Y.: Wilson, 1983), 203.
3. Harry Mazer, "Two Boys from the Bronx" (unpublished essay, 1995), 1–2; hereafter cited in text as "Two Boys."
4. "Mazer, Harry," in *Something about the Author,* vol. 31, ed. Anne Commire (Detroit: Gale Research, 1983), 127.
5. Harry Mazer, "A Huge Appetite for Books," *Scholastic Voice,* 18 October 1979, 15.
6. *Books I Read When I Was Young: The Favorite Books of Famous People,* ed. Bernice E. Cullinan and M. Jerry Weiss (New York: Avon, 1980), 113.
7. Harry Mazer, letter on writing *I Love You, Stupid!* (unpublished, no date).
8. Commire, 127.
9. Harry Mazer, transcript of speech to Illinois School Librarians, Champaign, Ill., 16 October 1986; hereafter cited in text as Illinois Librarians.
10. Commire, 128.

2. Coming of Age: Separation

1. Tobi Tobias, review of *The Dollar Man, New York Times Book Review,* 17 November 1974, 8.
2. Ibid.
3. Robert Unsworth, review of *The War on Villa Street, School Library Journal* (January 1978): 62.
4. Tobias.
5. Ibid.
6. Commire, 130.
7. Ibid., 131.
8. Harry Mazer, *The War on Villa Street* (New York: Delacorte, 1978), 35; hereafter cited in text.
9. Harry Mazer, *I Love You, Stupid!* (New York: Crowell, 1981), 118; hereafter cited in text as *Stupid.*
10. Marianne Gingher, "A Boy Who Runs Meets a Girl Anxious to Catch Up," *Los Angeles Times,* 12 March 1988, sec. 5, p. 6.
11. Review of *The Girl of His Dreams, Publishers Weekly,* 14 August 1987, 106.

3. Coming of Age: Connections

1. Harry Mazer, "Random Thoughts for Would-Be Writers of Young Adult Books" (unpublished essay, no date).
2. Carolyn W. Carmichael, "Profiles of Talent: Norma Fox and Harry Mazer," *AEB* (April 1976): 203.
3. Commire, 127.
4. Ibid., 129.
5. Ibid., 130.
6. "Mazer, Harry," in *Contemporary Authors: New,* vols. 97–100, ed. Frances C. Locher (Detroit: Gale Research, 1981), 357.
7. Jim McPeak, review of *When the Phone Rang, VOYA* (December 1985): 321.
8. Harry Mazer, "The Last Mission: Truth and Fiction," *ALAN Review* (Fall 1980): 1; hereafter cited in text as *ALAN Review.*

9. Harry Mazer, *The Last Mission* (New York: Delacorte, 1979), 187–88; hereafter cited in text as *Mission.*

10. Harry Mazer, "Random Writings from Harry Mazer's Computer" (unpublished essay, no date).

11. Harry Mazer, *The Island Keeper* (New York: Delacorte, 1981), 164–65; hereafter cited in text.

12. Harry Mazer, *Who Is Eddie Leonard?* (New York: Delacorte, 1993), 25; hereafter cited in text as *Leonard.*

13. Lucinda Snyder, review of *Who Is Eddie Leonard? School Library Journal* (November 1993): 125.

4. Seeking an Identity

1. Harry Mazer, *Guy Lenny* (New York: Delacorte, 1971), 109; hereafter cited in text.

2. Carmichael, 203.

3. Judith Higgins, "Books for Children: The New Paperbacks" (review of *Guy Lenny*), *Teacher* (February 1973): 125.

4. Harry Mazer, transcript of speech to ALAN Workshop, St. Louis, Mo., November 1988; hereafter cited in text as ALAN Workshop.

5. Harry Mazer, *The Girl of His Dreams* (New York: Crowell, 1987), 207; hereafter cited in text as *Girl.*

6. Harry Mazer, *City Light* (New York: Scholastic, 1988), 187; hereafter cited in text.

7. Harry Mazer, *Hey, Kid! Does She Love Me?* (New York: Crowell, 1984), 183; hereafter cited in text as *Hey, Kid.*

8. Harry Mazer, "If I Were an English Teacher . . . , " *Connecticut English Journal* (Fall 1993): 121.

9. Harry Mazer, "Dear Reader" (unpublished essay, no date).

10. Carmichael, 205.

5. Tales of Survival and Suspense

1. Holtze, 204.

2. Carmichael, 203.

3. Cullinan and Weiss, 113.

4. Carmichael, 205.

5. Harry Mazer and Norma Fox Mazer, *The Solid Gold Kid* (New York: Delacorte, 1977), 5; hereafter cited in text as *Solid.*

6. Jack Forman, review of *The Solid Gold Kid, School Library Journal* (September 1977): 148.

7. Ibid.

8. Holtze, 204.

9. Harry Mazer, *When the Phone Rang* (New York: Scholastic, 1985), 28; hereafter cited in text.

10. Harry Mazer, *Someone's Mother Is Missing* (New York: Delacorte, 1990), 16; hereafter cited in text.

11. Harry Mazer, letter to Ron Buehl about *Snow Bound,* 10 July 1972 (unpublished).

12. Ron Buehl, letter to Harry Mazer about *Snow Bound,* 26 July 1972 (unpublished).

13. Paul Weinman, "Description of Tug Hill in Upstate New York," *NAHO* (Albany, N.Y.: New York State Museum of Science Service, 1970).

14. Harry Mazer, *Cave under the City* (New York: Scholastic, 1986), 152; hereafter cited in text.

15. Hugh Agee, review of *Cave under the City, ALAN Review.*

16. Jim McPeak, review of *Cave under the City, VOYA* (December 1986): 220.

17. Hanna B. Zeiger, review of *Cave under the City, Horn Book Magazine* (March–April 1987): 211.

18. Christine Behrmann, review of *Cave under the City, School Library Journal* (December 1986): 106.

19. Lorraine Douglas, review of *The Island Keeper, School Library Journal* (April 1981): 142.

20. Carmichael, 205.

6. Romantic Fiction for Male Readers

1. Gingher, sec. 5, p. 6.

2. Review of *Hey, Kid! Does She Love Me? Booklist* (1984): 1250.

3. Libby K. White, review of *The Girl of His Dreams,* *School Library Journal* (January 1988): 87.
4. Zena Sutherland, review of *The Girl of His Dreams,* *Bulletin of the Center for Children's Books* (January 1988): 95.
5. *Booklist,* 1250.
6. Gingher, sec. 5, p. 6.
7. *Publishers Weekly,* 106.
8. Harry Mazer, *The Dollar Man* (New York: Delacorte, 1984), 86; hereafter cited in text.

7. Harry and Norma:
Relationship, Romance, and Writing

1. Norma Fox Mazer, interview with author, 3 March 1985; hereafter cited in text.
2. Norma Fox Mazer, "I Love It! It's Your Best Book!" *English Journal* (February 1988): 27.
3. Ibid., 26.
4. Jack Forman, review of *The Solid Gold Kid, School Library Journal* (September 1977): 148.
5. Nancy Vasilakis, review of *Heartbeat, Horn Book Magazine* (September–October 1989): 630.
6. Trish Ebbatson, review of *Heartbeat, School Library Journal* (June 1989): 124.
7. Zena Sutherland, review of *Heartbeat, Bulletin of the Center for Children's Books* (July–August 1989): 280.
8. Ebbatson.
9. Vasilakis.
10. Cindy D. Codell, review of *Bright Days, Stupid Nights, School Library Journal* (July 1992): 90.
11. Harry Mazer and Norma Fox Mazer, *Bright Days, Stupid Nights* (New York: Bantam, 1992), 126–27; hereafter cited in text.
12. Stephanie Zvirin, review of *Bright Days, Stupid Nights, Booklist* (June 15, 1992), 1826.
13. Zena Sutherland, review of *Bright Days, Stupid Nights, Bulletin of the Center for Children's Books* (May 1992): 242.

8. Harry Mazer: A Writer for Generations of Teenagers

1. David Peck, *Novels of Initiation: A Guidebook for Teaching Literature to Adolescents* (New York: Teachers College Press, 1989), xx.
2. "Harry Mazer," in *Contemporary Authors: New Revised Series,* vol. 32, ed. James G. Lesniak (Detroit: Gale Research, 1991), 289.
3. Richard Peck, "Some Thoughts on Adolescent Literature," *News from ALAN* (September–October 1975): 6.
4. Commire, 128.
5. John Yandell, "Just Sixteen: Teenage Fiction," *New Statesman and Society* (January–June 1990): 35.
6. Peck, xxi.
7. Lloyd Alexander, transcript of speech to National Council of Teachers of English (November 1982).
8. Lesniak, 288.
9. Commire, 128.
10. Harry Mazer, "On Surrendering Ourselves," in *Literature for Today's Young Adults,* ed. K. L. Donelson and A. P. Nilsen (Glenview, Ill.: Scott, Foresman, 1989).
11. Harry Mazer, quoted by Yamil Berard, "Author Recalls Story Behind Banned Book," *Fort Worth Star-Telegram,* 1 March 1995, 1B.
12. Mark I. West, "Censorship in Children's Books: Authors and Editors Provide New Perspectives on the Issue," *Publishers Weekly,* 24 July 1987, 109.
13. Ibid.
14. Harry Mazer, "Dear Yamil Berard," letter about article in *Fort Worth Star-Telegram* (9 March 1995).
15. Harry Mazer, letter on writing *I Love You, Stupid!* (unpublished, no date).
16. Harry Mazer, "Dear Charlie," 3 April 1995 letter to the author.
17. Harry Mazer, "Dear Charlie," 2 October 1995 letter to the author.

Selected Bibliography

Primary Works

Novels

Bright Days, Stupid Nights (with Norma Fox Mazer). New York: Bantam, 1992.

Cave under the City. New York: Crowell, 1986.

City Light. New York: Scholastic, 1988.

The Dollar Man. New York: Delacorte, 1984.

The Girl of His Dreams. New York: Crowell, 1987.

Guy Lenny. New York: Delacorte, 1971.

Heartbeat (with Norma Fox Mazer). New York: Bantam, 1989.

Hey, Kid! Does She Love Me? New York: Crowell, 1985.

I Love You, Stupid! New York: Crowell, 1981.

The Island Keeper. New York: Delacorte, 1981.

The Last Mission. New York: Delacorte, 1979.

Snow Bound. New York: Delacorte, 1973.

The Solid Gold Kid (with Norma Fox Mazer). New York: Delacorte, 1977.

Someone's Mother Is Missing. New York: Delacorte, 1990.

The War on Villa Street. New York: Delacorte, 1978.

When the Phone Rang. New York: Scholastic, 1985.

Who Is Eddie Leonard? New York: Delacorte, 1993.

Articles and Speeches

"A Huge Appetite for Books." *Scholastic Voice,* 18 October 1979, 15.

"If I Were an English Teacher . . . *Connecticut English Journal* (Fall 1993): 121.

"The Last Mission: Truth and Fiction." *ALAN Review* (Fall 1980): 1.

"On Surrendering Ourselves." In *Literature for Today's Young Adults,* 3d ed., edited by K. L. Donelson and A. P. Nilsen. Glenview, Ill.: Scott, Foresman, 1989.

Speech, ALAN Workshop, St. Louis, Mo. Unpublished (November 1988).

Speech, Illinois School Librarians, Champaign, Ill. Unpublished (16 October 1986).

Unpublished Letters and Random Writings

"Dear Charlie." Letter to the author about *Presenting Harry Mazer.* Unpublished (3 April 1995).

"Dear Charlie." Letter to the author about *Presenting Harry Mazer.* Unpublished (2 October 1995)

"Dear Reader." Letter to his readers. Unpublished (no date).

"Dear Yamil Berard." Letter to the author of an article in the *Fort Worth Star-Telegram* about Mazer's *The Last Mission.* Unpublished (9 March 1995).

Letter about writing *I Love You, Stupid!* Unpublished (no date).

Letter to Ron Buehl about *Snow Bound.* Unpublished (10 July 1972).

"Random Writings from Harry Mazer's Computer." Unpublished (no date).

"Random Thoughts for Would-Be Writers of Young Adult Books." Unpublished (no date).

"Two Boys from the Bronx." Unpublished (1995).

Secondary Works

Behrmann, C. Review of *Cave under the City. School Library Journal* (December 1986): 106–07.

Berard, Y. "Author Recalls Story behind Banned Book." *Fort Worth Star-Telegram,* 1 March 1995, 1B.

Carmichael, C. W. "Profiles of Talent: Norma and Harry Mazer." *AEB* (April 1976): 203–206.

Codell, C. D. Review of *Bright Days, Stupid Nights. School Library Journal* (July 1992): 90.

Cullinan, B., and M. J. Weiss, eds. *Books I Read When I Was Young: The Favorite Books of Famous People.* New York: Avon, 1980, 113.

Douglas, L. Review of *The Island Keeper. School Library Journal* (April 1981): 142.

Ebbatson, T. Review of *Heartbeat. School Library Journal* (June 1989): 124.

Forman, J. Review of *The Solid Gold Kid. School Library Journal* (September 1977): 147–48.

Gingher, M. "A Boy Who Runs Meets a Girl Anxious to Catch Up" (review of *The Girl of His Dreams*). *Los Angeles Times,* 12 March 1988, sec. 5, p. 6.

Higgins, J. "Books for Children: The New Paperbacks" (review of *Guy Lenny*). *Teacher* (February 1973): 125.

"Mazer, Harry." In *Contemporary Authors,* vols. 97–100, edited by F. Locher, 355–58. Detroit: Gale Research, 1981.

"Mazer, Harry." In *Contemporary Authors: New Revised Series,* vol. 32, edited by J. G. Lesniak. Detroit: Gale Research, 1991.

"Mazer, Harry." In *The Fifth Book of Junior Authors and Illustrators,* edited by S. H. Holtze, 203–04. Bronx, N.Y.: Wilson (1983).

"Mazer, Harry." In *Something about the Author,* vol. 31, edited by A. Commire, 126–31. Detroit: Gale Research, 1983.

Mazer, Norma Fox. "I Love It! It's Your Best Book!" *English Journal* (February 1988): 26–29.

McPeak, J. Review of *Cave under the City. VOYA* (December 1986): 220.

———. Review of *When the Phone Rang. VOYA* (December 1985): 321.

Peck, D. *Novels of Initiation: A Guidebook for Teaching Literature to Adolescents.* New York: Teachers College Press, 1989.

Review of *The Girl of His Dreams. Publishers Weekly,* 14 August 1987, 106.

Review of *Hey, Kid! Does She Love Me? Booklist* (1984): 1250.

Snyder, Lucinda. Review of *Who Is Eddie Leonard? School Library Journal* (November 1993): 125.

Sutherland, Zena. Review of *Bright Days, Stupid Nights. Bulletin of the Center for Children's Books* (May 1992): 242.

———. Review of *The Girl of His Dreams. Bulletin of the Center for Children's Books* (January 1988): 95.

———. Review of *Heartbeat. Bulletin of the Center for Children's Books* (July–August 1989): 280.

Tobias, T. Review of *The Dollar Man. New York Times Book Review,* 17 November 1974, 8.

Unsworth, R. Review of *The War on Villa Street. School Library Journal* (January 1978): 62.

Vasilakis, N. Review of *Heartbeat. Horn Book Magazine* (September–October 1989): 630.

Weinman, P. "Description of Tug Hill in Upstate New York." *NAHO.* Albany: New York State Museum and Science Service, 1970.

West, M. I. "Censorship in Children's Books: Authors and Editors Provide New Perspectives on the Issue." *Publishers Weekly,* 24 July 1987, 108–11.

White, L. K. Review of *The Girl of His Dreams. School Library Journal* (January 1988): 86–87.

Yandell, J. "Just Sixteen: Teenage Fiction." *New Statesman and Society* (January–June 1990): 35.

Zeiger, H. B. Review of *Cave under the City*. *Horn Book Magazine* (March–April 1987): 211–12.

Zvirin, S. Review of *Bright Days, Stupid Nights*. *Booklist* (15 June 1992): 1826.

INDEX

149

The Author

Arthea (Charlie) Reed is the Director of Development and Education for Northwestern Mutual Life–Asheville. She was the chairperson of the Department of Education at the University of North Carolina at Asheville from 1989 to 1995. A professor of education from 1978 to 1996, she has taught courses in adolescent literature, English methods, foundations of education, and research. She has written an adolescent literature textbook for future teachers (*Reaching Adolescents: The Young Adult Book and The School,* Merrill, 1994) and a trade book for parents (*Comics to Classics: Books for Teens and Preteens,* Penguin, 1994). In addition, she has written several other books in the field of education, including *In the Classroom: An Introduction to Education* (Dushkin, 1995) and *A Guide to Observation and Participation in the Classroom* (Dushkin, 1995). She is coeditor of the Penguin USA teachers' guide series and is the author or a coauthor of many of the guides on classic books. Recently, she has been editing and writing teachers' guides for classic books on CD-ROM.

Charlie Reed is the 1995–1996 president of ALAN, the Adolescent Literature Assembly of the National Council of Teachers of English. She was editor of the *ALAN Review* from 1984 to 1990. She has been honored by her faculty colleagues at UNCA for her teaching, scholarship, and service by being named the 1985–86 Feldman Professor. Charlie Reed has taught at every level, from elementary through graduate school, in four different states.

Reed lives on a mountaintop near Asheville, North Carolina, with her husband, two dogs, and a cat. For relaxation, she likes nothing better than to hike on the trails near her mountain home.

The Editor

Patricia J. Campbell is an author and critic specializing in books for young adults. She has taught adolescent literature at UCLA and is a former Assistant Coordinator of Young Adult Services for the Los Angeles Public Library. Her literary criticism has been published in the *New York Times Book Review* and many other journals. From 1978 to 1988 her column "The YA Perplex," a monthly review of young adult books, appeared in the *Wilson Library Bulletin*. She now writes a column about controversial issues in adolescent literature for *Horn Book* magazine. Campbell is the author of five books, among them *Presenting Robert Cormier*, the first volume in the Twayne Young Adult Author Series. In 1989 she was the recipient of the American Library Association's Grolier Award for distinguished achievement with young people and books. A Native of Los Angeles, Campbell now lives on an avocado ranch near San Diego, where she and her husband, David Shore, write and publish books about overseas motor-home travel.